This can be completed by the owner, or perhaps in pencil by someone else if the book is a present!

Model:

Registration number:

Colour:

Extras:

When purchased:

Distinguishing marks/dents/scratches etc:

Condition: Excellent ☐ Good ☐ Fair ☐ Bad ☐ Unloved ☐ Other ☐

Most memorable experience in the Jaguar:

Longest journey:

Best passenger:

Worst passenger:

Jaguar club membership:

Other Jaguars you'd most like to own:

Any other comments:

Photograph:

JAGUAR

DRIVER'S BOOK

A **FOULIS** Motoring Book

First published 1990

Published by:
Haynes Publishing Group
Sparkford, Nr Yeovil, Somerset BA22 7JJ

Haynes Publications Inc.
861 Lawrence Drive, Newbury Park, California 91320 USA

British Library Cataloguing in Publication Data
Ruppert, James
  Jaguar driver's book.
  1. Cars
  I. Title
  629.2'222
  ISBN 0-85429-626-3

Library of Congress catalog card number 89-85906

US softback edition ISBN 0 85429 847 9

Editor: Mansur Darlington
Page layout: Chris Hull & Alan Hobday
Printed in England by: J.H. Haynes & Co. Ltd

Contents

FORE WORD

To freely confess to once having had a passionate love affair with a motor car, could I suppose invite an investigation into one's moral and physical condition by worried relatives. But I did have such an encounter and it was, to say the least, a smouldering relationship.

It happened quite a few years ago when financial ruin often stared me bleakly in the face. At the time, I tottered about in a venerable Morris saloon that was so old, it had a secret passage in the boot, and it didn't have a handbrake . . . it was a pike staff.

When that noble metal patriarch finally wheezed into a death-like state in Ormskirk, I cursed life roundly and vowed never to give my heart to another saloon car, especially one that required a major service at Lourdes. But of course fickle fate or whatever, saw things in a very different light, and one morning as a watery sun bled its feeble rays over a Manchester abbatoir complex, in a car showroom . . . I fell hopelessly, head over heels in love with a second-hand Jaguar XJ6. It lay in wait; throbbing like Blake's tiger "Burning Bright."

Her paintwork shone and glittered . . . the loveliest blue I had ever seen; the bumpers sparked off fragments of shimmering atoms . . . To hell with ruin . . . I had to possess that Jaguar.

There is no point in going on about how I got my hands on the car, suffice it to say that I did without actually creating a crime wave to raise the cash. (Although frankly, at one stage I thought seriously of selling two of my kids for the deposit). That Jag and I were lovers; we purred the lanes together, we roamed the hills together and we darted through traffic like minnows together. That first Jaguar of mine gave me four years of unbridled bliss before juddering to a halt one night in Bayswater, never to move a sprocket again. I've run Jags for years, I love 'em but I swore I'd never show my emotions so openly, and I meant it . . . But now in my garage there is a 1973 12 cylinder fixed head "E" Type . . . Here I go again.

*I*NTRO *D*UCTION

Whether it's fresh out of the showroom, or a ropey MOT borderline it's still a Jaguar, and for most people that means style, luxury, speed and value for money. Yet owning a Jaguar says more about you than cash ever can. As a Jaguar owner or enthusiast it at least proves that you've got taste.

• Jaguar have of course had some pretty hard times, especially during the '70s, but the good news is that things have changed.

Now they're World Sports Car Champions, Le Mans winners again and have successfully launched the XJ 40 and are looking forward to an even brighter future. Jaguar, it seems, are back where they belong.

I hope you enjoy reading The Jaguar Driver's Book because that's the intention. You'll even find a Jaguar Trivia Test at the back to make sure that you've been paying attention.

In researching this book I have tried to dig up interesting and unusual cars, owners and facts. I haven't always succeeded. One of my failures was an XJS that looked like a prop from a Mad Max film going in the opposite direction one Sunday afternoon. I swung round and chased after it but couldn't catch up. Perhaps I was dreaming. Perhaps I was suffering from 'Jaguar Fever'. Whatever it was, that owner can contact me for inclusion in The Jaguar Driver's Book II, whatever world he, she or it came from.

So if you like reading about, laughing about and just looking at Jaguars, start turning the pages now!

James Ruppert

ThanX...

Without other people willing to put up with your tiresome phone calls, endless letters and constant requests for photographs and information, a book like this would be rather thin. So here they are, the people who really need all the thanks.

Dee for her patience and encouragement. Mr B. Johns of D.J. Sportscars. Mr Guy Salmon of Guy Salmon. Richard Stewart of Robin Hood Cars, R.G. Stevens Kougar Cars, Paul Atterton at Sotheby's. Bridget Tedds, Roger Clinkscales and David Waring at Jaguar Cars. Nigel Byles. Duncan Hamilton Limited. Proteus Reproductions. Jeremy Russ at TWR. Daryll Group at The History of Jaguar Museum, a brilliant place to visit. Jeffrey Levitt at Mint and Boxed. Laurence Pearce at WP Automotive. Peter Hall of the Industrial Control Services. Jon Pressnell at *Autocar*. Janspeed Limited. Dave Rogers. Derek Robinson at Triple C Challenger. Anthony Taylor at Autotune. Hilary Davis at Handmade Films. Michael Mitchell at Lynx. Peter Keiselt. Mr and Mrs. Winter at Silhouette Cars. Jaguar Drivers Club. John Ridley at the Daimler and Lanchester Owners' Club. Graham Searle at the Jaguar Enthusiasts Club. Panther Cars and the Panther Owners Club. Phil Street at Trent Engineering. Nicholas Goldthorp at Vicarage Cars. Martin Nott at *XJR Magazine*. Malcolm Bryan, Ottercraft Limited. Jaguar Car Club. Rob Iles and Rod Grainger at Haynes. Mum and Dad for all their help. And finally all those authors who've written about Jaguars before, Philip Porter, Paul Skilleter and in particular the late Andrew Whyte. And also thanks to anyone I've shamelessly left out, I hope they know who they are.

Unless otherwise indicated all photographs are from the Jaguar Archive, the author's own collection, or supplied by featured companies. If any photos are not covered by those terms, both the author and publisher would be interested to hear from the copyright holder.

THE *Jaguar* HERITAGE

What's the connection?

It's hard to believe now, but the first "Jaguar" was actually attached to a motorcycle. What the Swallow Sidecar shared with today's high performance XJs is quality, value for money and good looks. Those were the qualities that William Lyons, and later Sir William, abided by throughout Jaguar's history.

The Birth of Swallow

In 1921 Lyons was just an ambitious car salesman and enthusiastic motorcyclist when a certain Thomas Walmsley became his neighbour in Blackpool. Walmsley shared a passion for motorcycles and possessed a truly magnificent combination.

The Swallow sidecar was hand built by Walmsley and sold privately in modest numbers. William Lyons was an early customer who also saw the business possibilities and was just twenty when the partnership was formed. The Swallow Sidecar Company came into being in 1922. Both men had judged the marketplace correctly and the demand for their sidecars grew, and so did the company. By 1926 they were also producing hoods and side curtains for motor cars. In addition Swallow sidecars became more refined, offering increased weather protection.

Cars

Lyons didn't want to stop at producing sidecars and accessories, especially since he had purchased an Austin Seven and found the specialist fabric bodywork to be very fragile. Lyons knew that Swallow could do better. In early 1927 the company managed to obtain an Austin Seven chassis and by the

spring the Austin Seven Swallow was announced.

The original Austin Swallow photographed with its hard top in place, an option never offered by any other manufacturer. At first, production was slow, no more than two cars a day. Soon after, the much larger Morris Cowley Swallow sports two-seater was introduced. And as their coachbuilding skill and reputation increased they added further chassis to the range. By the time of the 1929 Olympia Motor Show they included FIAT, Swift and Standard amongst others. The short-lived Fiat 509A, the popular Standard 9 and the rare Wolseley SS. Lyons and Walmsley also moved Swallow to much bigger premises in Coventry where Jaguar have remained and prospered until today.

In spite of the coachbuilding success Lyons still wanted to produce a complete Swallow car. By forging close links with Standard, a completely new model was born.

The SS1 was the toast of the 1931 Motor

Show. It cost only £310 but was described as having the £1,000 look. But incredibly it wasn't the car that Lyons had wanted the public to see, because he had envisaged a much lower look. Having been in hospital with appendicitis his partner Walmsley had given the car the go ahead. Not content, after just 500 examples had been built Lyons got his own way and in 1932 introduced an SS1 with a lower roofline.

With such internal conflicts it's probably not surprising that the two men went their separate ways. Walmsley left in 1934 to pursue other interests, which even included caravan manufacture.

Profile: William Walmsley

Early Years

Entered family Coal Merchants after school. Interest in coachbuilding stemmed from making railway coach bodies and coal carts for the business.

The sidecars

Popularity with the opposite sex is cited as one reason why Walmsley turned his attention to building a sidecar. With his brother-in-law Fred Gibson and sisters Blanche, Molly and Winifred he produced the first prototype, nicknamed 'Ot-as-Ell.' The rest, as they say, is history.

11

After SS

15 years after that first sidecar, Walmsley left to pursue other business interests. This included the design and manufacture of luxury caravans.

Sum up

Unfortunately Walmsley is the forgotten man of Jaguar. Yet without his sidecars, who else would have inspired Lyons to enter motor production?

SS Jaguar

Lyons was now free to develop a totally new model and to this end he assembled a team of specialist engineers. The results were seen in 1935 and was their first four-door saloon.

The new name

People were not sure what SS stood for. Some remembered the Swallow and others Standard. It was almost called a Sunbeam, but Lyons lost out to Rootes who eventually acquired the marque. The advertising agency suggested that a strong identity was needed. It was agreed that a powerful animal would be the ideal figurehead. One animal kept creeping to the top of their list. The name that Lyons finally chose was Jaguar. The famous mascot was an optional extra.

Milestone models: SS Jaguar 100

Birth

A development of the very limited production SS90.

Technical

The 100 had a conventional design, but featured the advanced Weslake overhead-valve cylinder head.

Speed

In $3^1/_2$ litre form the 100 as its model name indicated, could easily reach 100 mph. This made it the company's first genuine 'ton up' car.

Nickname

And with the $2^1/_2$ retailing for just £395 and $3^1/_2$ for only £445, Lyons had yet again built an astonishing car at an incredible price. Jealous motorists gave the 100 a nickname, "The Wardour Street Bentley".

Sport

Jaguar regarded it simply as a fast tourer which was primarily aimed at competition. In fact, the 100 earned Jaguar its first true racing victories, starting with the 1937 Vila Real (Portugal). In the hands of privateers, the 100 continued to be successful well into the post-war years.

Legacy

The Jaguar 100 has come to embody the spirit of the 1930s sportscar for many enthusiasts. It is also the inspiration behind many of today's replica kit cars. But most importantly, it established the Jaguar sporting creed that the XK models would soon follow.

When in 1937 SS went over to all steel construction there were some production difficulties as new skills were needed to cope with this new type of manufacture. The result was a car that had even better ride and handling characteristics than before.

War service

Progress was halted when war was declared in 1939, although Lyons made sure that they weren't idle.

SS became official repairers of Whitney aircraft as well as manufacturing parts for many other famous British aircraft, which included the Stirling, Mosquito, Spitfire and Lancaster. Later in the war they also assembled the first British jet aircraft, the Gloster Meteor. The demand for the Swallow sidecar though, had not abated. In all, something like 10,000 were built up until 1945 specifically for the War Department. Like the rest of Coventry, SS suffered bomb damage, but they always managed to re-start production.

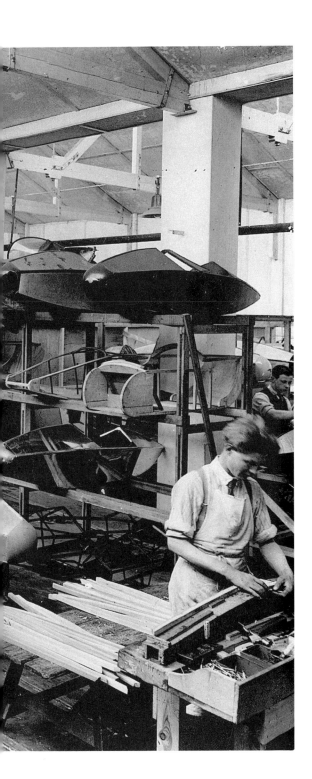

Production progress

This is the body shop in Foleshill Coventry about 1929. Not long after their attention had turned to Swallow cars. In the late '40s the pre-war range was re-badged as Jaguars. *Overleaf:* 1957 and the sad and charred remains inside Brown's Lane after the great fire. Ten years later E-Type and saloon production is at full tilt, attempting to satisfy the incredible demand.

Jaguar Cars

As the war came to a close in 1945 an important announcement was made, SS Cars would now be known as Jaguar Cars Ltd. This was a reflection of the success of the pre-war range of cars and to disassociate itself from the infamous German organisation of the same name. In this post-war period materials were scarce and the first cars to be badged as Jaguars were the old SS saloons and coupés, although the SS 100 never reappeared. During the war Lyons and his engineering team when on fire watch duty would also use that time to discuss and design the new Jaguars. However an all new Jaguar did not appear until 1948.

Export or else

The Mark Five was a large saloon aimed primarily at the all important North American market. In the "export or die" climate of the time, those manufacturers who aimed their products abroad got a higher steel allocation. So Lyons used all this extra metal to chromium-plate the window frames, fit double front bumpers and rear wheel spats. Two tone paintwork and drophead body styles were all introduced specifically for our rich cousins over the pond. But the toast of the first post-war Motor Show in 1948 was the new Jaguar sports car.

What was originally planned to be a stop-gap model rapidly became the most desirable sports car of the forties and fifties. The XK 120 (capable of over 120 mph!) had an all new twin-camshaft engine which had been developed for the next generation of Jaguar saloons. Whilst production for the saloon was delayed, a shorter chassis was produced and clothed in a beautiful two seat body. Coupé and drophead coupé body styles soon followed.

Milestone models XK 120

Why?

The Jaguar Super Sports Car was its first designation and that wasn't far wrong. Originally conceived as a test bed for the new generation of twin-camshaft XK power units, events dictated that the roadster would enter production almost as a stop gap measure.

How?

Tooling for the big new Jaguar saloon was delayed, which gave Lyons the opportunity to produce a short wheelbase version of that chassis. Upon that powerful platform was placed one of the most beautifully sculptured sports cars of all time.

Production

There were enough orders taken at the 1948 Motor Show to justify full scale production, rather than the hand assembly that had

originally been planned. Yet again Jaguar scored on price. The basic model retailed at just £998. And for that you got a 120 mph top speed and a 0–60 time that was under 10 seconds.

Sport

The XK 120 was almost bred for competition and scored an impressive string of inter-national rally victories throughout the '50s. Not surprisingly it formed the basis for the Le Mans conquering C and D types that followed.

Legacy

Thanks to the XK 120, Jaguar was back on the sporting map. Gradually the XKs became more refined, the XK 140 in 1954 and XK 150 in 1957 were increasingly roomy and practical, although an XK 150S was offered in 1959 with a 3.8 litre engine and blistering 135 mph performance.

Saloons

Jaguar saloons were also setting the pace in the 1950s. The Mark VII, VIII and IX proved that a large luxurious saloon could also handle like a sports car. The 2.4 of 1955 had unitary construction, graceful bodywork and kept tradition with all previous Jaguars by offering tremendous value for money. Prices started at just £1,344.

Royal approval

Exports were up and both premises and workforce were growing. In recognition of this success Her Royal Highness the Queen visited the Brown's Lane factory. But just a year later on February 12th 1957 tragedy struck when fire swept through the building. It is a tribute to Jaguar that just 36 hours later cars were coming off a shortened production line. Sadly the exciting new XKSS sportscar that had just been introduced would never reappear. But Jaguar were not to be put off from announcing another new model, the 3.4 saloon, on February 26th.

The sixties

Jaguar entered the sixties with the 2.4 and 3.4 in classic Mark II guise and with several new models on the way, amongst them the big Mark X which is the direct ancestor of today's XJ6. There were also strong rumours that a spectacular sports car was on its way to replace the XK 150. That car was of course, the E-Type.

Milestone Models: E-type

Birth

Originally conceived as a replacement for the competition bred D-type. However, Jaguar officially withdrew from racing in 1957 which meant that the E-type was developed from a racing car into a road going sports car.

Impact

"The Greatest Crumpet-Catcher Known to Man" was how a journalist chauvinistically described Jaguar's brand new sportscar in 1961. The E-type was a car that just couldn't be ignored. Like the XK 120, its impact on the motoring world was sensational.

Performance

Malcolm Sayer's design was simply breathtaking, a natural development on the racing D-type's lines. In fact, the E-type was a genuine racer capable of speeds in excess of 150 mph.

Features

All round disc brakes, independent suspension and powerful XK engine wrapped in a beautiful body.

Price

And the few cars that could match that performance, certainly couldn't come close on price, with the roadster costing just £1480.

USA

In order to meet the American import regulations the E-type evolved into the Series 2 and 3s and for many lost its early appeal. But right up until the V12 powered roadster in 1974, the retail price never rose above £4,000!

Legacy

The E-type is a car that symbolises the sixties. The definitive sports car and the definitive Jaguar.

Diversification

Jaguar did not restrict themselves to building

glamorous sportscars. In 1960 Jaguar acquired the oldest British motor manufacturer, Daimler. As well as allowing Jaguar to add a famous name to their range of cars, it also provided much needed production capacity and diversification into bus and even armoured car (The Ferret) manufacture. A year later the liquidated truck builders Guy, joined the Jaguar Group and once revitalised produced a new range of trucks and tractors called the Big J or "Big Jaguar." In 1963 Coventry Climax was added to the Group and brought much valued engineering expertise to the company.

Birth of the XJ6

Although Jaguar appeared to be successful their range needed to be rationalised. They were offering four engine sizes, four saloon styles, with badge engineered Daimler versions as well, not forgetting the convertible, coupé and 2 + 2 E-types. The demand was there, but for a relatively small manufacturer, the supply wasn't. However, the XJ6 was intended to remedy this situation and lead the world in luxury saloon design. Lyons also hoped that a merger between the British Motor Corporation (BMC) and Jaguar would provide the support that was needed. These two momentus events, the model launch and BMC merger occurred in the same year, 1968.

Milestone models: XJ6

Special

The sports saloon category was virtually invented by Jaguar. With the XK engine, the post-war saloons were both powerful and

agile. In 1968 the new car that effectively replace the existing range, had to be something special. Fortunately the XJ6 was up to the task.

Performance

Beneath the beautiful yet traditional body lurked the chassis and power unit of an E-type, in the 4.2 version. Not surprisingly the performance and handling was outstanding.

Prizes

Car of the Year Award soon followed in 1969 repeated in 1972 with the XJ12. Anti-dive suspension won Jaguar the 'Don' Safety Award.

Development

Over subsequent years the car received only minor face lifts in '73 and '79 which

confirmed the strength of the original design. There's probably only one thing better than an XJ6 saloon and that's the coupé. The classic lines became even more beautiful once the door pillar was removed on the Series 2 model.

Legacy

The XJ6 has proved to be Jaguar's most important model ever. A consistent export earner which has provided a base for the company's revival.

BMC, BL and all that

Jaguar as part of this large group was beginning to lose its identity, particularly after Sir William Lyon's retirement in 1972. The final blow was struck in 1975 with the nationalization of British Leyland. For many, this was a year of disappointments. At the Motor Show Jaguar was part of the "Leyland" stand and announced their new sportscar, the XJS. The XJS was a very different car from the E-type, more of a Grand Tourismo than out and out sports car. It was offered in just one 2 + 2 bodystyle, which itself attracted much criticism because of the so-called flying buttresses. And inside the dark cockpit there wasn't even any wood veneer on the dashboard!

The mid to late seventies were dark times for Jaguar. Production was up, but quality was down and complaints from the UK and the important North American market increased. Not only that, nationalization had frozen much of the in-house design and development work. But there is a happy ending, you'll just have to wait until the end of the book, that's all!

Profile: Sir William Lyons

Early Years

William Lyons was born on September 4th 1901 in Blackpool. At school he preferred sports to more serious academic work. When it came for him to start work, his father, who ran a small music shop, arranged for young William to become a trainee.

Into the car business

Lyons had entered the motor industry with Crossley Motors. But for the ambitious Lyons the company did not offer him the challenges, or prospects that he needed. However, his passion for motorcycles brought him into contact with many other enthusiasts. One of them was Jack Mallalieu who managed a local Sunbeam franchise and Lyons went on to join Mallalieu's new business as a salesman. It was then that the Walmsleys moved nearby with their fascinating sidecar combination.

Achievements

He was knighted in the 1956 New Year's Honours List. Responsible for the design and development up until the XJ6. Need anymore be said?

Personal qualities

Not surprisingly a great leader with an ability to motivate whilst delegating to a trusted group of deputies. The low sleek lines of the Jaguar are entirely attributable to Lyons. Often he would secrete himself in some quiet corner of the factory with a few panel beaters to translate his classic designs into metal.

Postscript

In 1972 at the age of 70 he retired. On the 8th February 1985 Jaguar's founder died at Wappenbury Hall which had been his home for more than half a century. But he had lived long enough to see his company flourish again and give his approval to the new XJ40 in its final pre-production form.

The Daimler Heritage

When they bought Daimler in 1962, Jaguar not only increased their engineering expertise, they also acquired a valuable piece of British motoring history. Frederick Simms, acknowledged as the 'Father of British Motor Industry', met Gottlieb Daimler, producer of the first 'real motor car', at the Bremen Exhibition in 1890. An agreement was reached and the Daimler Motor Syndicate was formed in 1893 and registered as the Daimler Motor Company in 1896. British versions of the German Daimler initially rolled out of a converted cotton mill in Coventry.

From its inception, Daimler achieved many firsts.

* The Prince of Wales, later King Edward VII, was the first Royal to go on a 'motorised journey' in a Canstatt-Daimler that belonged to Simms.

* The first car to successfully complete the route from John O'Groats to Land's End in 1897 was of course a Daimler.
* And the world's first fluid flywheel and pre-selector self-change gear was introduced across the Daimler range in 1930.

But as well as being a favourite amongst the Royals, Daimler also diversified into areo engine and commercial vehicle production. This led to Daimlers in many guises performing active service during the First and Second World Wars.

Jaguar derived Daimler or Daimler derived Jaguar?

That's the friendly debate that still continues today between enthusiasts of the two marques. Certainly both companies have exerted a positive influence on one another but when Jaguar took over Daimler in 1962 they inherited two very different cars and an outstanding engine.

The V8 story

Daimler's range consisted of the fibre-glass bodied 2^1/$_2$ litre SP 250 sports car and the luxurious 4^1/$_2$ litre Majestic Major limousine. Both cars were powered by lightweight V8s. For Jaguar, the engine provided a marvellous opportunity to boost the performance of their existing models. When the unit was installed in a Mark 1, it all but transformed the car. Performance was instantly improved because the engine produced 140 bhp (20 hp more than Jaguar's XK 2.4). And being very light, weight distribution was much better which made the Jaguar's handling even more responsive.

However, the unit could not be adopted across the Jaguar range, as production in quantities large enough to be cost effective was impossible. So it was decided to install the engine into the Mark 2 bodyshell. The result was the Daimler 2^1/$_2$ V8.

Outwardly the new car was very similar to the Jaguar, apart from the fluted radiator, numberplate light and a twin exhaust system. Under the skin though, the Daimler had its unique engine, softer suspension, a lower rear axle ratio and on the inside there was more luxurious trim and thinner front seats meant more rear legroom. The Daimler had a top speed of 110 mph, as against 96 for the Jaguar, although it cost just £100 more.

The first badge engineered Daimler appeared in 1966 and was based on the Jaguar 420. The Sovereign was powered by the 4.2 XK unit, but the flutes, 'D' badges and name on the camshaft covers remained.

The Daimler 2^1/$_2$ was renamed the V8 250 and along with the Jaguar 240/340 range received slimmer bumpers and new hub caps, but retained its front fog lamps.

Daimler Limousine

Daimler did manage to establish its own identity again even it if was courtesy of a Jaguar 4.2.

The opposition

Within the BMC group at the time were several competing models in the prestigious limousine market such as the Austin Princess, Jaguar Mark X and Daimler Majestic Major.

The decision

It was decided to design an all new car that would be the perfect limousine.

The Introduction

In 1966 whilst all the other models were phased out, the Daimler limousine was introduced.

The Limo

Based on the 420Gs running gear and stretched floor pan. With its excellent rear legroom, headroom and capacious boot, the limousine proved to be an instant success.

27

Sum up

No Mayor or celebrity can afford to be seen without one.

The V8 250 continued in production until 1969 when the XJ6 based Sovereign took over. From then on, every Daimler has effectively been a Jaguar, but with an extra touch of luxury that makes it special.

JAGUARS IN COMPETITION

To many people, Jaguars are first and foremost sports cars. They might build sensible four-door luxury saloons, but at the heart of those machines beats a refined, but high performance engine. Jaguar's racing pedigree is not in doubt, but their direct involvement in motor sport has been very sporadic.

Early years

The mating of the lightweight Swallow body to the Austin Seven chassis made the SS a popular choice amongst racing enthusiasts at hill climbs and trials all over the country. The SS saloons that followed offered more scope for competition and Lyons saw the potential. In 1933 five specially prepared tourers (three of them painted red, white and blue), with bumpers removed and a wheel on each wing were entered for Europe's toughest rally, the Alpine. Three of the cars went on to finish, the highest placing was 14th.

The SS was finding success in the Concours d'Elegance classes rather than high overall placings in the endurance trials. But the arrival of the SS100 sportscar began to change all that.

SS100 in competition

In the 1936 Alpine trial the 2.7 litre SS Jaguar of Tommy Wisdom and his wife Elsie, had a penalty free event and the result was SS's best Rally performance to date. This lead to the SS Jaguar being taken more seriously as a performance car by motoring enthusiasts all over Europe.

Lyons appreciated the negative effect of racing failure and on some occasions even persuaded private entrants to withdraw when the competition looked a bit too stiff! However, the standard SS Jaguars could take on the great cars of the day, such as BMW and Aston Martin and still win.

International

There was a class win at the 1936 Marne Grand Prix. Outright victory at the 1937

Portugese Vila Real which was the first international victory. Whilst at home the more humble Welsh Rally provided another outright victory. What also gave Jaguar immense satisfaction in 1938 was the new all steel SS Jaguar Saloon's first prize in the Grand Prix d'Honeur class of the 1938 Monte Carlo Rally. Although the car only finished 42nd over the stage, the award was a testament to the new saloon's refinement and quality. It could only boost sales.

USA

A private owner, Paul Marx even took an SS100 to the United States to compete in racing events, long before Jaguar took E-types and XJRs to do battle!

Post-war

In the immediate post-war days it was the SS100s that were dusted down and entered in hill climbs and the like by private owners. In 1948 though, Ian Appleyard proved the car's worth with an outright victory in the Alpine Rally.

XK 120 in competition

Only with the arrival of the XK 120 in 1948 did Jaguar seriously consider re-entering the racing arena. The first post-war production car race at Silverstone saw Jaguar score a convincing 1-2 victory in the new XKs. Inspired by this success Jaguar prepared more cars for competition use and in the 1950 Mille Miglia finished a creditable fifth. In the Le Mans event of that year two XK's finished in mid field. This proved to be valuable experience for their assault on the next year's event. But before then, they scored a famous victory at the Ulster Tourist Trophy with a young Stirling Moss at the wheel. Appleyard also began to amass Alpine Cups and many other rallying victories.

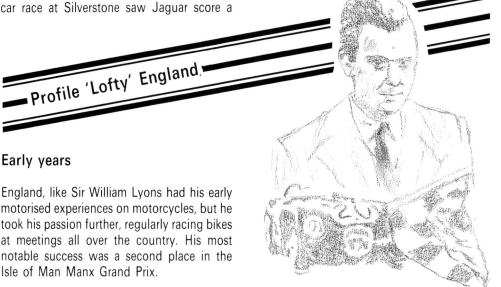

Profile 'Lofty' England.

Early years

England, like Sir William Lyons had his early motorised experiences on motorcycles, but he took his passion further, regularly racing bikes at meetings all over the country. His most notable success was a second place in the Isle of Man Manx Grand Prix.

Racing

His engineering expertise was gained as an apprentice at Daimler in London. Whilst there he also scored his first competition success finishing second in the 1931 RAC rally in a customer's car, presumably with the customer's permission! Stints at Alvis, Whitney-Straight and E.R.A., where he looked after Dick Seaman, Britain's most successful pre-war racing driver, increased his practical knowledge.

Le Mans

In 1946 England was appointed Jaguar Service Manager, but it was no surprise in view of his considerable experience that he was placed in charge of their competition activity. England masterminded Jaguar's famous five Le Mans victories in the fifties. Promotion to Service Director in 1956 was a recognition of his considerable contribution to the company's success in the post-war period.

Postscript

When Lyons retired in 1972, England was the obvious successor, although they were troubled times for Jaguar. He retired just two years later aged 62, having found the position of non-executive Chairman difficult under the prevailing Leyland management.

The big saloons

The Mark Five surprised everyone by being an agile Monte Carlo Rally performer coming 3rd in '51 and fifth in '53. Most notable was the performance of the works Mark Seven saloons in the Monte Carlo Rally. In 1955 they won the team prize with outright victory being achieved the following year. The Mark Seven also did well on the race track with five successive Silverstone touring car race wins, from '52 to '56.

Jaguar drivers in the '50s

Undoubtedly the golden era for Jaguar, they nurtured many for the world's finest drivers. The cockpit of a C or D-type produced some of Britain's best sportsmen, Whitehead, Walker, Flockheart . . .

Ian Appleyard: Proved himself in the post-war years as one of the world's best rally drivers. Winning the 1948 Alpine Trial in a 1930s 100! On many occasions he was partnered by his wife Pat (Sir William Lyons daughter). Further Alpine Cups followed in XK 120s '50, '51, '52, '53 and the RAC Rally in 1953.

Stirling Moss: Probably the most famous and professional of British racing drivers. His first win was in an XK 120 at the 1950 Tourist Trophy. And before Formula One became his main priority Moss also drove C-types to victory at Reims and again at the '51 TT, including many fine placings. Although he never won Le Mans in a Jaguar, he did finish second in 1953.

Mike Hawthorn: One of the true flamboyant characters in '50s motor racing. The high point of his association with Jaguar was the 1955 Le Mans victory with Ivor Bueb. He was borrowed back from Ferrari in 1958 to test drive the prototype E-type.

Ivor Bueb: Known as 'Ivor the Driver' Bueb lived up to his name. Being reliable, professional and above all fast, he scored two Le Mans victories.

Jaguar and Le Mans

This is without doubt the most important race to Jaguar. Some say that it has been an obsession, but in the 1950s it was nothing short of domination. This makes it possible to trace the conception and development of Jaguar's most famous sports cars in relation to the race.

C-type: development

By the autumn of 1950 work on a Jaguar Racing car had begun. There was nothing wrong with the engine and gearbox of the XK 120 but weight had to be reduced, handling improved and brakes uprated. In short this would be a car capable of winning Le Mans.

Name

Originally the new car was to have been called the XK 120C, the 'C' standing for competition, but it finally became known as the C-type.

Technical

The new chassis was made out of lightweight steel tubing. The bodywork was sleek with a combined front wing and bonnet section that hinged forward.

Performance

Lighter weight and lower drag meant that 100 mph could be obtained on 20% less power than was required by the XK 120. After testing, the C-types made their debut at the 1951 Le Mans.

1951

For a time the cars maintained a commanding 1-2-3 lead, but engine failures left just one Jaguar in the race. The lone Jaguar however, was way ahead and won at a record speed of 93.498 mph. This was the first British victory at the Le Mans event since 1935.

1952

The C-types were distinguished by new and more aerodynamic nose and tail sections. It had been intended to use these modifications in the following season, but the new streamlined Mercedes 300 SL posed a potentially faster threat. This new design though led to severe overheating problems and the retirement of all the Jaguars.

1953

Not surprisingly for the following year's event a thoroughly tested and revised car did appear with the addition of an air intake on the bonnet for the carburettors.

Jaguar's success and domination of the 1953 Le Mans was total. Tony Rolt and Duncan Hamilton's C-type had a 30 mile lead when the chequered flag fell that afternoon. In second and fourth places were the other works C-types, with a Belgian owned Jaguar finishing ninth. A civic reception awaited the teams return to Coventry.

D-type

October of 1953 saw Jaguar introduce a stunning prototype with what was described as a "bubble" over the driver's cockpit. This eventually became the D-type and appeared at the 1954 Le Mans. It had in fact been ready for the '53 event, but Jaguar had paid the price in 1952 by entering an untried car.

Technical

The D-type was a logical development of the C and incorporated some advanced features. Most notably there was no separate chassis, the D-type being the first monocoque construction racing car. It was light and very aerodynamic with a distinctive wrap around windscreen and large tail fin. Power had also been boosted to 250 bhp.

1954

At their Le Mans debut, one retired with a blocked fuel line, another in the hands of Stirling Moss, suffered a 160 mph brake failure, although he survived unharmed. Jaguar had to be content with a second place to Ferrari. Public demand for the D-type was so great that Jaguar modified the cars for limited production.

1955

The works cars now featured a longer nose, improved wrap around screen, and Weslake designed cylinder head which now meant a true top speed of almost 185 mph. Le Mans that year was a tragic one, when eighty spectators were killed by a crashing Mercedes. The battle between the Jaguars and Mercedes 300 SRs ended when the Stuttgart Directors withdraw their cars. Jaguar went on to win the race, although some claimed that it was a hollow victory.

Retirement

Although Jaguar officially withdraw from competition in 1956, factory prepared and assisted D-types were still entered at Le Mans and other sports car races.

1956

Although having to keep within fuel restrictions and other regulations Ecurie Ecosse team fielded a team of D-types. However on lap 2, both Fairman and Frère spun their cars and retired, whilst Hawthorn's car developed a misfire. Flockhart and Sanderson went on to win in their D-type whilst a Belgian entered Jaguar came fourth and Hawthorn sixth.

1957

Jaguar again! 1st Flockhart and Bueb Ecurie Ecosse 3.8 2nd Scottish entered 3.4 of Sanderson and Lawrence 3rd French entered D of Lucas 4th Equipe Nationale Belge car of Rouselle and Frère 5th 3.8 D-type of Hamilton and Gregory.

1958

Hamilton and Bueb led ,for a ,while but crashed in heavy rain. The Ecurie Ecosse cars both retired with piston failure.

1959

Ecosse Ds retire with engine failure.

E-type

Intended as the racing successor to the D, the E2A was the competition equivalent of the prototype E1A, although both had all alloy construction. The 'A' stood for aluminium.

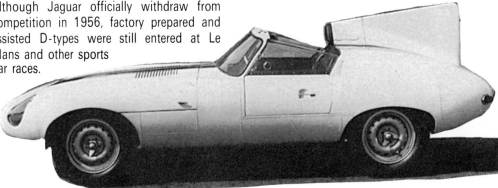

The racer

It looked similar to the D because it retained the tail fin and full width screen that were part of the regulations. The engine was also restricted to 3.0 litres to keep within the rules. A first for Jaguar was the independent rear suspension.

1960

E2A prototype was entered by the American enthusiast Briggs Cunningham. For a time it held on to ninth place before retiring with engine failure. Ecosse D-type also retired with engine trouble.

1961

No Jaguar at Le Mans.

1962

Modified standard coupés of Cunningham and Salvadori finished fourth with Sargent/ Lumsden Car fifth.

The Lightweight

This racing E-type had an aluminium body and engine block, which saved 500 lbs over the standard car. 3.8 litre unit was reinstated, fuel injected with wide angle cylinder head, high lift camshaft, dry sump lubrication and special ZF five-speed gearbox.

1963

Briggs Cunningham fielded three of these lightweights, but only he managed to finish the race in 9th position.

1964

Two 'E's entered but they both failed to finish. There would be a 20 year gap before Jaguar returned.

1985

Group 44 again. Tullius in the XJR-5 finished 13th.

XJRs

Jaguar never abandoned thoughts of building a car specifically for the race track. The Group 44 team responded to Jaguar's enthusiasm by producing a V12 car for the IMSA (International Motor Sports Association) category for prototype racing. It was called the XJR-5 and was effectively an American built Jaguar! or Jagwah.

XJR-5

Designed by Michigan engineer Lee Dykstra. Featured steel bulkheads, aluminium honeycomb floor, and a glass fibre semi-monocoque body.

1984

Group 44 Team brought two XJR-5s. Both cars failed to finish.

1986

XJR-6 TWR placed in charge of the Jaguar team for Group C, they had rejected the American chassis and 48 valve head power unit in 1985. These were replaced with a lighter 24 valve V12 and a brand new structure designed by Tony Southgate. The TWR XJR-6 failed to finish.

1987

Three XJR-8LMs this time. For a while the three cars did manage to maintain a 1-2-3 formation, but the superiority of the Porsches began to show. At 3am Win Percy's Jaguar suffered a rear tyre failure and flipped on the Mulsanne Straight. Not much was left of the car, but Percy walked away from the wreckage. After sixteen hours Nielsen brought in the second Jaguar with cylinder head damage. The last car spun, needed a gearbox rebuild, had electrical problems, and a new suspension upright. But in spite of all this, it still managed to finish 5th.

The three survivors with Car 2 on its victory lap.
(Picture Malcolm Bryan).

1988

The XJR-9LM of Jan Lammers, Johnny Dumfries and Andy Wallace returned the Le Mans crown to Jaguar after 21 years. They won by the slimmest of margins, just under three minutes, making it one of the most exciting races in Le Mans history. Lammers was the strongest starter as he chased after a pack of Porsches, never dropping below second place and after the 14th hour holding the lead until the end. The American crewed XJR-9s of Derek Daly, Kevin Cogan and Larry Perkins finished fourth with Danny Sullivan, Davy Jones and Price Cobb in fourteenth. Jaguar were back!

39

■ Profile Tom Walkinshaw ■

Early years

What had begun as a hobby, racing MG Midgets, was turned into a successful business, Tom Walkinshaw Racing, or TWR as the company is more commonly known. TWR has now become the competitions arm of Jaguar, being able to offer the attention and specialist expertise that a major manufacturer finds difficult to provide.

Racing

Even before his involvement with Jaguar, Walkinshaw was racing the BMW 3.0 CSLs that dominated saloon car racing in the '70s. In fact, he witnessed at first hand the shortcomings of the Broadspeed XJ Coupés as they failed in competition.

XJS

The announcement of the new Group A rules for touring cars in the 1982 season, where engine and body modifications would be restricted convinced Walkinshaw that the XJS would be perfect. Although, John Egan listened they could only offer moral support for the time being. At the end of that season there were four outright wins, with a third and fourth overall placing in the championship.

Championship I

For the following seasons Jaguar's profile, not surprisingly, became higher and their support more evident, which culminated in the outright Championship win of 1984 with Walkinshaw at the wheel. The first Jaguar win in this event for 21 years.

XJRs

When the decision was made to campaign a car in the Group C events it was Walkinshaw who took the intiative and commissioned the XJR-5 which then received the full backing of Jaguar.

Championship II

With the XJR-6 in 1987 Walkinshaw returned Jaguar to worldwide prominence, although he wasn't at the controls, by winning the World Sportscar Championship.

Le Mans

Jaguar's dreams come true in 1988 with a win. Walkinshaw said it would take three seasons to crack and he was right.

Jaguar drivers in the '60s

Jaguar's official participation in motorsport had ended, but there were still private enthusiasts like Briggs Cunningham, John Coombs and Roy Salvadori, to name just a few and some other very familiar names. *Graham Hill:* He is probably best known for his Formula One victories, but Hill came from an age where drivers raced literally anything. He campaigned many Jaguar cars including Mark IIs and taking an E-type to its first competition victory at Oulton Park in 1961. *Jackie Stewart:* Jaguar saloons virtually marked the start of Stewart's incredibly successful racing career which of course culminated in World Championship victories. What helped him on his way was the family Jaguar franchise!

The Mark 1 & 2s

These took over from where the Seven left off, being particularly effective in rallies. In 1959 3.4s won the Tulip, Tour de France and the Monte Carlo team prize. The cars went on winning in 3.8 guise with Alpine Cups '60 and Tour de France '60–'63. On th track the 3.8 Mark 2 was the first European Touring Car Champion. It remained competitive until the mid-sixties, when the large American cars and Lotus Cortinas took over.

The E-type

The last competition E-type, or Jaguar of any sort in the sixties was built in 1966. But in the hands of private entrants Jaguar's presence on the race track was maintained. It was British Leyland, of which Jaguar were a reluctant part, who officially returned the E-type to competition. Leyland backed the V12 in the North American racing events, in

order to promote the marque in that lucrative marketplace. In the hands of Bob Tullius the V12 became National Champion for 1975.

Jaguar drivers in the '70s

Barren years for Jaguar, although of course the cats were still comon sights at historic and club meetings. Amongst the flag wavers were: *Bob Tullius:* American Tullius deserves a special place in racing history for keeping the Jaguar name alive in competition through the '70s. At the wheel of a V12 E-type he became National SCCA Class B champion in 1975. More recently he has piloted the XJR-6 and 7s, finishing a creditable 13th at the '85 Le Mans.

Derek Bell: One of Britain's most versatile drivers, he raced the powerful but ill fated XJ12 coupés. He has won Le Mans, but only for the opposition and that means P*****E. Perhaps he'll return to Jaguar and XJRs in the near future before he retires.

The XJ12

For 1976 and 1977 Leyland campaigned in the Group Two Europeans Race Championship with the XJ12 Coupé. Prepared by Broadspeed the cars had tremendous power (500 bhp), but an absolute lack of reliability. On its debut at the Silverstone Tourist Trophy, Derek Bell powered into the lead before finally breaking a drive-shaft. In fact,

they led every single race they took part in and at the end of '77 the cars had just a second and fourth placing to show for their efforts. Perhaps one more season would have seen them tasting success.

The XJS

In the States the Group 44 team who had been so successful with the E-type applied the same principles to the XJS. Race winning results soon followed throughout the late seventies and early eighties. But in Britain the XJS was not used as a serious competition tool until 1982. Tom Walkinshaw of TWR assessed the possibilities and guessed that the XJS in mildly modified form stood a good chance against the reigning BMWs. He was proved right when the TWR-Motul XJS won four major races that season. As a result they got full works backing for the 1983 season, then winning the Championship outright in 1984.

Jaguar drivers in the '80s and '90s

The '80s revival is virtually due to the faith and skill of one man, Tom Walkinshaw. With the XJS he proved that Jaguar could win again. Now in the '80s and '90s he's getting some more help. However, with the expansion of the XJR team there are almost too many drivers to choose from. But here are a few who have made their mark.

Raul Boesel: This Brazilian really made a name for himself when he became the World Sportscar Champion in 1987. Starting successfully in Formula 3 he had several Formula 1 drives before finishing his feat in sports prototypes. For the 1988 season he took care of Jaguar's IMSA commitments in the USA.

Johnny Dumfries: Also known as the Earl of Dumfries, he won the 1984 British Formula Three Championship and moved on the Formula One with Lotus in 1986. Drives with Sauber-Mercedes, Porsche 962 and a victory in '87 in an XJR-8 led to a full time place in

'88. Career highlight so far must of course be the Le Mans win.

Jan Lammers: Considered by many to be one of the finest endurance drivers around, he proved it in 1988 by leading Jaguar to victory at Le Mans. He only became a regular team in driver '87 having raced a Group C car in 1985.

Martin Brundle: Formula 3 success led eventually to Formula 1 drives for Tyrrell and Zakspeed. In between these outings he drove both Group A and C cars for Jaguar and had the distinction of leading the field in the marque's first ever race. In 1987 he commited himself to a full season, scoring four wins in five races and finishing third in the Championship. Consistent driving in 1988 brought him the driver's title.

John Watson: Well known for his Formula 1 activities including several fine wins, he moved sideways into sportcars. In '84 he joined the Group 44 team at Le Mans although neither XJR-5 finished. After switching to Porsche in 1986 he finally partnered Lammers a year later in the XJR-8. 1987 was a good year, three victories, equal second in the Driver's Championship and an award for being the most successful British racer in a British car abroad.

World Champions

On two occasions Jaguar had come close to winning the World Sports Car Championship in both 1953 and 1955. By the end of the season, Jaguar had a 2 point lead over Ferrari in the World Sports Car Championship with just one race to go. However, Jaguar pulled out of the Carrera Panamericana, probably because South America was too far to go, leaving Ferrari to win. A similar thing happened in '55 when the last event was the Targa Florio, where few British manufacturers ever competed. But by the '80s the Championship was now for teams rather than makes and the rules were very different.

1985: TWR were put in charge of Jaguar's assault on Group C (defined as 'two seater competition automobiles built specially for races on closed circuits) Championship. Although the team was only able to compete in five of the ten Championship races, their debut at Mosport in Canada was impressive. Whilst the leading XJR-6 went on to retire, another car claimed second place.

1986: The only real highlight of the season was the popular win at the Silverstone 1000 km, although the team did finish 3rd in the Championship.

1987: As many improvements were incorporated in the XJR-6s design for the season the models were re-designated as XJR-8s. They won at Jarama, Jerez, Monza, Silverstone, Brands Hatch, Nurburgring, Spa-Francorchamps and Fuji. This was enough to decisively wrest the Championship away from Porsche, it also made Raul Boesel the Drivers Champion. Not only that, Jan Lammers, John Watson and Eddie Cheever were 2nd, 3rd and 4th respectively.

1988: An indication that things might be different that season was the surprise Mercedes win at Jerez in Spain whilst the Jaguars had gearbox trouble. However, TWR proved that they could easily bounce back at Jarama, Monza, Silverstone and Le Mans. Despite Mercedes comebacks at Nurburgring and Spa, Lammers and Brundle's second at the former event was enough to clinch the title again for Jaguar. The icing on the cake, was Martin Brundle winning the driver's title.

Sum up

Jaguar's 50's racing heyday has returned.

In between tyre changes Jaguar won at Fuji. (Picture Malcolm Bryan).

PERFORMANCE JAGUARS

Is there such a thing as a slow Jaguar? Probably not. Even the earliest Swallows succeeded in putting a streamlined and lightweight body on top of the existing chassis, which often meant more mph.

XKSS – the hairiest Jag?

The cars were created to use up the spare D-type bodies produced to meet racing regulations. To keep out the weather a mohair hood was provided, along with detachable sidescreens. On the inside leather trim **added** a touch of refinement to the otherwise full race D-type. But if you have any luggage, hard luck, there's no boot, just a luggage rack.

Not surprisingly as it's a D-type the performance is electrifying. 0–60 in a shade over 5 seconds and capable of at least 150 mph. At the moment there's no production Jaguar that can better those figures.

Now has all that whetted your appetite for a faster Jaguar?

Coombs Jaguar 3.8 One of the most potent performance Jaguars was offered by Coombs Garage. John Coombs the racing driver was behind it all. The modifications included lightened flywheel and gas flowed heads. On this car you can also see that the wheel arches have been cut away and slightly flaired to give the tyres more breathing space. (Photo Courtesy Sotheby's).

XKSS When Duncan Hamilton fitted his ex-works D-Type with a windscreen and hood in 1956, he created one of the fastest road Jaguars ever. The factory's version followed soon after, the only modifications being that the division between driver and passenger was removed, a door installed on the nearside, a full width windscreen with surround, quarter bumpers and a side mounted exhaust.

XK 150S This had a Weslake cylinder head, three carburettors, with 9:1 compression pistons, lightened flywheel and strengthened clutch. The result was 250 bhp and 136 mph. The small 'S' below the quarterlight distinguished it from the standard car.

XK 120 With this model Jaguar began to tinkering with the performance potential of their cars. The special equipment pack included 8:1, or 9:1 compression pistons, rejetted carburettors, high lift camshaft, dual exhaust, lighter flywheel and a solid centre clutch to deal with the extra 20 bhp. This pack was also made available on the Mark VII saloons. No slow coach in its own right by increasing the big car's performance, Jaguar had effectively invented the luxurious sports saloon.

Lynx performers

Every Lynx performer is individually prepared to the customer's own specification, which include the following options:

TURBO 3.6 Lynx exhaust/manifold, large inter-cooler, high compression pistons and modified engine management unit.

TURBO 4.0 AJ6 engine, balanced, blue-printed and bored to 4.0 litres. Lynx gas flowed cylinder head, high compression pistons, modified camshaft, large displacement turbo system, dash mounted electronic variable boost control and a revised engine management system for optimum performance and efficiency.

V12 Specially designed and profiled camshafts, full gas flowing with high efficiency inlet manifold and large bore exhaust system.

Arden Biturbo

What Arden do to a standard XJ 3.6 to make it into a 330 bhp 249 km/h saloon is the following. They add two racing tested IHI Superchargers. An additional injection jet supplies the exact quantity of fuel needed according to the boost pressure and rpm. There is also a high performance exhaust system made of NIROSTA steel. And for 12-cylinder XJs they can also supply a five-speed manual gearbox. Enough said?

Janspeed turbo

Whilst everyone waits for the V12 engine to be made available in the XJ40, Janspeed have plugged the gap in the market with a twin turbocharger conversion. The RotoMaster RM60 water-cooled turbochargers are regulated by Rajay modular wastegates, mounted on special steel exhaust manifolds. The Janspeed Jaguar produces 293 bhp which powers the car to 60 mph in just over 6 seconds and on to a top speed of 140 mph.

Lister XJS

Hand-built from the shell upwards, this is a totally reworked Jaguar with the power boosted to 6.0 litres, which means more than 400 bhp and a top speed that should nudge 170 mph.

To achieve this performance the engine is completely modified with steel conrods, forged pistons, gas flowed and polished heads, 11.7:1 compression ratio, Cosworth valve springs, lightweight followers, reprofiled camshafts, induction system and reprogrammed fuel management system. A five-speed Getrag gearbox makes everything even more exciting, although an uprated GM400 automatic gearbox is also available.

And to keep all this on the road the suspension has been stiffened with gas filled shock absorbers amongst other modifications that can be tailored to the customer's own requirements.

Lister XJ 40

To boost the XJ 40's top speed to 140 mph, Lister modify the engine by installing a longer throw steel crankshaft which increases the engine's stroke to 102 mm. The conrods and pistons are changed, along with the gas flowed and polished cylinder head.

And to handle the extra power the suspension is lowered and strengthened. Wider three-piece Lister wheels and Pirelli P700 tyres increase the grip.

Turbo Technics Jaguar XJ6 3.6

One of the most respected names in turbo charging have turned their attentions to the Jaguar range.

A pair of water-cooled Garrett T25 turbos increase power output from 220 bhp to a massive 299 bhp. The turbos are mounted on new exhaust manifolds and the existing fuel injection system is uprated with an additional injector. An intercooler adds power whilst promoting cooler operating temperatures.

The 0–60 mph time is slashed by 2 seconds to 6.5 and it will reach 100 mph in just 18 seconds. Top speed is in excess of 145 mph.

·J·A·G·U·A·R·S·
With A Difference

If you want to add that personal touch to your Jaguar there are plenty of options, from fitting spoilers, or calling in a coachbuilder for something more drastic, to actually taking the Jaguar to bits and starting all over again.

The choice is all yours.

Arden body kit

This Streamline Spoiler Set has been developed in a wind tunnel and not only provides better aerodynamics, but also supplies cooling air to the mechanical parts that matter. Therefore the disc brakes and engine compartment benefit from a constant circulation of fresh air. But never mind that, looks dead flash doesn't it?

Lynx Eventer

How do you make an XJS look good from all angles? Well you can either cut the roof off, but Jaguar have already done that, or turn it into an estate car. This is Lynx's successful attempt to make the XJS more stylish and practical.

To make all this happen they've added a new roof section and strengthened the body, whilst redesigning the fuel tank to fit below the floor. Inside, the Conolly hide rear seats conveniently split. Lockable compartments keep valuables out of sight.

Lynx Spyder

If you can't afford Jaguar's XJS convertible, then the Spyder is the answer. Rather than take a hacksaw to your old model, Lynx will use heavy gauge fabricated steel sections to strengthen the body. An electrically operated hood keeps your physical exertions to the minimum. Automatic rear quarter lights complete the open air picture.

Guy Salmon XJS Jubilee

To celebrate 50 years of retailing Jaguars, Guy Salmon decided to produce a unique range of modified XJSs. The example pictured has a roof and boot spoiler, front and rear aprons, side skirts, colour coded bumpers, twin headlights, chrome radiator with additional grille and a return of the leaping Jaguar, this time gold plated! Inside there is a wood-rim steering wheel with matching walnut centre console, gear lever knob and radio panel. Not bad for a birthday present!

Twenty Six

As the brochure for this remarkable limousine proclaimed, "twenty six inches make all the difference." Guy Salmon linked up with Glenfrome Coachbuilders to produce a car in which you could really stretch your legs, however long they are. The creature comfort list is impressive, colour television, video, fridge, cocktail cabinet, walnut occasional tables . . . etc. Although one option at just £275 is absolutely essential, a Kleenex tissue dispenser!

Half breeds?

What do you do with a rusty Jaguar? Cry? Take it to the scrapyard? Spend a small fortune on a restoration? Or drive it until it falls apart? Well those heart rending decisions need not arise if most of the running gear is in order. The alternative is to build a Jaguar based kit car.

When it comes to Jaguar kits you're almost spoilt for choice, but they broadly fall into two categories:
1. Those that look like classic Jaguars.
2. Those that don't.

Steadman TS 100

How about an SS Jaguar 100 look-alike? Who can resist those classic '30s lines? That's why Ottercraft have recreated the shape in aluminium alloy panelling. The windscreen also folds flat to reveal two aero screens for proper 'wind in the hair' motoring.

The chassis is a combination of the original design and contemporary strengthening modifications. Wax oiling and plastic mounts between the bodywork and steel chassis dramatically reduces the chances of corrosion.

Based on the XJ6, finding a donor car, of whichever series won't be difficult. Steering rack, brakes, engine, gearbox and differential can all be utilised, with a degree of mix and match for a 'customised' result.

The TS 100 can be bought complete or acquired in a partially finished state for the buyer to finish. This is a true blast from the past tempered with the refinement and practicality of today's modern Jaguars.

Proteus "C" & "D"

If you want to feel like a Le Mans winner everytime you slip down to Tesco for the shopping, make sure that you take a Proteus reproduction with you.

The cars come either complete, or in component form so that you can fit the remaining Jaguar parts. Any six-cylinder XK engine is suitable from 2.4 to 3.4. The D's body is made entirely from aluminium, whilst the C is a combination of aluminium and glass fibre.

Lynx D-type

As coachbuilders, Lynx have managed to transform the XJS range. Their skills have also been applied to building what are regarded as the best Jaguar replicas. Indeed, the Lynx D-types are almost as sought after

as the real thing! The high prices they command also bears this out.

The Ds are available in either short, or long nose form and even as a soft top XKSS model.

Aristocat

This is a kit made within the spirit of the XK series whilst not attempting to be an exact copy of the XK 120. Consequently this is a more practical and up-to-date car.

The Aristocat is based on either the component parts of an XJ6 or XJ12. The kit itself can be collected in stages, to spread the cost and save space, or as a complete car. The basis is a spaceframe chassis whilst the body is made from glass fibre.

Working with Jaguars on a day to day basis means that the makers, Autotune, have produced a car that is easy to assemble and above all, fun to use.

Challenger E-type

To get hold of an original Series 1 E-type Roadster you'll need an awful lot of money, or a very understanding bank manager. But if all you've got in the world is an XJ6 with a body that's seen better days, then the Challenger is the answer.

It's possible to buy the Challenger in various states of completion. And as the basic kit comes with all the important panels fitted, finishing the job to a high standard shouldn't be difficult.

Telling the Challenger apart from the real thing isn't easy as it roars past you. Triple wiper blades and other reproduction pieces of chromework add to the authenticity.

Dax Tojeiro

DJ Sportscars International were specialists in all forms of glass reinforced plastic manufacture for many years before they turned their hands to building cars in 1982.

The inspiration for their kit came from the legendary AC Cobra designs of the sixties. John Tojeiro is now their technical director, but not only was he the designer of the AC Ace, forerunner of the Cobra, he also built those superb racing Tojeiro Jaguar's of the '50s. What makes these connections something more than a coincidence, is that Tojeiro joined the company only after driving one of their cars.

The Dax Tojerio is based around the XJ Jaguars and will accept both the six-cylinder and V12 power units, as well as suspension and ancillary equipment. There is a choice of chassis, either standard platform, or competition 'supertube.' And a choice of body, '289', or '427.' These combinations can also be purchased in cost effective stages, which leaves some of the work up to you.

Expert opinion suggests that with a Jaguar V12 engine, this is even better than the real thing.

RS Daytona Spyder

It apparently took Robin Hood Engineering four years research to get this Ferrari replica right and the result is extremely impressive. If you've got an XJ6, XJ12 or S type, then this Italian supercar can be yours in several stages of finish, from partly built to a complete vehicle.

The body is glass fibre, but the rest of the specification conforms almost exactly to the original Ferrari, right from the basic dimensions to the mohair hood. You'll be hard pressed to tell this apart from the original.

Apart from being the centre of attention in this Daytona, you'll also find that Jaguar parts and servicing is guaranteed to be cheaper!

Ronart W152

If you thought that real sports cars weren't made anymore then the Ronart will make you think again. The W152 resembles the classic Formula 1 cars from the '30s, '40s and '50s.

The S6 version is powered by the XK 4.2 unit and the V12 version has the 5.3 litre engine. Brakes and modified suspension also come from the Jaguar.

Like the old cars it imitates the W152 has a separate steel chassis. But as well as modern reliable Jaguar mechanics the body is manufactured from Kevlar, which is the latest composite fibre material (an aluminium body is available to special order).

The only problem with the Ronart is, where do you put the luggage?

GGW 456J

Kougar Sports

Imagine what a Jaguar powered Morgan would be like and you'd probably end up with something that closely resembles a Kougar Sports. As it has no doors the Kougar brings back the days of good old 'hop in' motoring, providing you're still fit enough to do it.

Based on the S-type's running gear, the glass fibre body is bonded straight onto the chassis for added strength. And with such a light (18 cwt) package, the performance is quite astonishing. The engine options range from 3.4, 3.8 to 4.2.

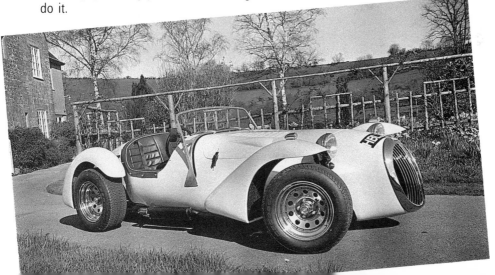

Silhouette SC 5000S

Now if you really wanted to turn heads what could be better than a Countach? And what could be better than one with a Jaguar V12? The performance is almost that of the real thing, but you'll also save a great deal of money in the process.

The chassis are jig built for strength and clothed in a hand laminated fibreglass bodyshell. It is possible to buy the SC 5000S in varying stages of completion, from the body kit through to, chassis, suspension and completely assembled car.

Behind the wheel of an SC 5000S you'll never go unnoticed again. And that's a guarantee.

Vicarage Mark 2

At first it sounds too good to be true, a brand new Mark 2 Jaguar saloon. But in an age where cars have lost their character and seem about as hand crafted as plastic cutlery, the Vicarage Mark II comes as a breath of fresh air.

However, Vicarage are more than just Jaguar restorers. Their cars are re-engineered to the highest standards which means that the handling and performance characteristics bear comparison to modern vehicles.

To get some idea of the time and dedication that goes into building a Vicarage car lets look at a summary of how they're built.

1. Vicarage find a basically sound Mark 2, although the car needn't be totally complete or even running.
2. The body is then stripped to a bare shell.
3. The shell is then blasted with $1^1/2$ tons of shot to remove all of the rust and paintwork.
4. Any unsound areas are cut away and replaced with hand made steel panels.
5. The now perfect shell is treated with a zinc chromated primer and an acrylic twin-packed primer. And also to fight rust the chassis sections are wax-oil injected prior to assembly with the underside treated with seam sealer and stone chip resistant coatings.
6. The body is then carefully hand sprayed in the desired colour to produce a lasting sheen. So far 480 hours have been spent on the Vicarage.
7. Every chrome part is new or re-chromed.
8. The braking system is rebuilt with perishable items replaced. All other parts are shot blasted, zinc plated and stove enamelled.
9. Rack and pinion power steering from the XJS is used.
10. A specially designed rear independent suspension unit is installed.
11. The engine and gearbox is stripped and rebuilt.
12. The clutch, cooling system, stainless steel exhaust, wiring loom, weather seals and wire wheels are all brand new.
13. Inside everything is fully retrimmed. Sound-deadening pads are fitted to the floor and across the bulkheads beneath the new deep pile carpets. All the door panels are renewed and Conolly hide is used on the upholstery. The walnut woodwork is re-veneered and lacquered.
14. The final touch is two days of polishing before a comprehensive road test and pre-delivery inspection.

Vicarage future: At the time of going to press a convertible Mark 2 and a Vicarage E-Type were projects close to fruition.

Before you buy

When new, Jaguars represent incredible value for money, offering performance, luxury and refinement that the competition find hard to match. Where else would you get a highly polished veneer dashboard, serenely powerful engine and the envious glances of other motorists. As a used proposition a Jaguar is potentially the best motoring bargain around. However, you must choose your Jaguar carefully, a mistake can prove to be costly.

Always set yourself a budget when buying your "new", old Jaguar and don't stray over it. You should also leave a few hundred pound cushion to cover "unexpected" expediture.

Servicing isn't cheap and neither are parts. Do it yourself mechanics can probably handle a service on the six-cylinder engines, but accomplished mechanics have been known to wilt at the daunting sight of the V12 power unit.

On recent models, a full service history is essential to guarantee that the Jaguar has been properly maintained.

Whenever you look at a used Jaguar, try and take a friend with you to act as an objective eye and ear, i.e. to catch things you miss. Never rush a decision, always go away and think about it. Always drive the car and make sure that you look and listen to its performance and appearance. Don't be rushed. If you ever have doubts about any aspect of the car, don't buy it! Believe me there's plenty more Jaguars that are just right for you.

The following selection of post-war Jaguar models serve as a general guide to their collectability and general durability with useful tips on what to look for.

The engine & mechanics

The XK units are very strong and well proven, but if neglected can cause problems.

Look where the car has been standing, or move it. Are there oil deposits?

Lift the bonnet and look inside. Examine the engine block as closely as you can, if not weather protected they do crack. Check the radiator and oil level. If any of these fluids have mixed the cylinder head gasket has probably blown. Start the engine from cold and listen for unwelcome noises from the timing chains, camshafts and tappets. Watch for excessive blue smoke from the exhaust, which can mean that the bores are worn. Once the engine is up to running temperature (with at least 40 psi oil pressure) use cloth to remove the oil cap. Smokey fumes will mean that the engine needs a good overhaul. Misfiring might be old plugs or incorrect points setting, or most seriously a stuck valve.

Noisy exhaust? Replacing them is very expensive.

For the V12 the checks are much the same, but it's important to realise that this is a much more complex unit. Repairs are expensive and beyond the DIY mechanic. But being aluminium the unit is more sensitive to abuse, which usually means that the head gasket has failed. Check the fluid levels and the condition of the engine and assess for yourself whether the car has been looked after.

Test drive

Power steering: With engine running turn wheel lock to lock, engine shouldn't falter or stall. Also pump the brake, revs should drop slightly.

Automatic transmission: With engine running apply brake and move gear selector through the D, N and R positions. There should be no audible 'clonks'. With brake still applied increase revs when in Drive or Reverse and car should rise at either end. On the road the transmission should respond smoothly. Have a look at the gearbox fluid, if dirty it indicates excessive wear.

On the drive: Listen for unusual rattles, creaks and knocks. Make sure that you investigate

them thoroughly, although it can just be some loose items in the boot. Driving over rough ground will often reveal any suspension weaknesses, such as excessive pitching.

The gear lever should move easily through

the gears. There should be no excessive noise in first or reverse gears. Make sure that overdrive, when fitted, will engage. Car should pull away without too much complaint in second, changing from second straight to top will reveal any clutch slip.

XK 120/140/150

Looking around

Tyres: Check for wear. If inside tread worn down this is an indication that the suspension needs attention.

Inside: Make sure that you try out all the 'toys'. If the heater and air conditioning don't work, putting them right can be very expensive. Electric windows must travel smoothly from top to bottom, as should sunroof. Carefully check the condition of the upholstery. Cracked, split or stained leather means an expensive re-trim. The same thing goes for damaged headlining and badly marked veneer on the dashboard.

Production history

The XK120 was available to the public from 1949 onwards. Body originally constructed from aluminium, replaced by steel in 1951. Special equipment performance options also offered. In the same year the fixed head coupé was offered. In 1953 the drophead coupé introduced. 'C' or competition cylinder head also available on range. Discontinued in the autumn of 1954.

XK140 replaces the 120. Engine moved forward 3" to make more cockpit space and rack and pinion steering introduced. Heavier Mark VII bumpers, new wider slotted grille, new rear lights, boot handle and medallion featuring Le Mans wins were the most obvious stylistic changes. Special equipment version had C-Type head.

XK150 introduced in spring of 1957. First car with four wheel disc brakes. Bodywork featured significant changes. Higher front wing line, wider grille, new bumpers, number

plate repositioned on boot, wraparound windscreen and leaping cat mascot offered as an extra. More room inside due to thinner doors. Performance option was the B-type head. Roadster version introduced in 1958. Triple carburettor 'S' available across range in 1958. XK150S roadster with 3.8 litre engine announced in 1959.

Mechanics

See earlier comments for XK units.

Bodywork

Look around the headlamps, sidelights, bottom of wings, footwell ventilators, door hinge/shut pillars, sills (feel underneath the body) and battery boxes (140 & 150) for rust or signs of repair. Check join between rear wings and top panel or coupé roof. If soft top, lift hood and check for rot. In the boot remove spare wheel and look everywhere for rust. Doors, bonnet and boot lid all rust. Be on the look out for bodges such as metal plates, filler and underseal. Check chassis and if you can, inspect the car from underneath.

Spares

Most mechanical parts are common and Jaguar cottage industry ensures that spares are constantly being remanufactured. Reproduction body panels are also generally available.

Comments & collectability

XK120 seen as most desirable with aluminium bodied rarest of all. Make sure that original before parting with huge sums of money. Right-hand drive XK140 roadster very rare. Prices for all models very high. Many American left-hand drive re-imports, not necessarily rust free.

Mark VII, VIII and IX

Production history

The Mark VII was introduced in 1950 and although a big car had quite sparkling performance because it shared the engine with the XK 120 sports car. It had a huge separate chassis. From 1952 the finish was improved by the adoption of synthetic enamel paint and improved sealing. In 1953 more efficient telescopic dampers uprated the suspension. Performance packages were also offered. These included modified pistons, distributors, carburettors and even a C-type cylinder head, as used on the competition cars. Overdrive became an option in 1954, the year it was discontinued.

The Mark VIIM had a much more powerful engine which was rated at 180 bhp. It also had a facelift which meant new headlamps, bumpers and wheel trims. In 1955 an automatic Borg-Warner gearbox was offered on the British market for the first time.

In 1956 the Mark VIII marked another power increase to 190 bhp. On the outside there was a chrome strip which separated the two-tone paintwork, a larger radiator and single, instead of split windscreen. It also became a more luxurious car, with rear picnic trays and improved seating.

For a time the Mark VIII was produced along with the new Mark IX which was introduced in October '56. This is explained by the fact that the IX had the new 3.8 litre XK engine. It had power-assisted steering and disc brakes all round. The VIII was discontinued in December 1969 and the IX in September 1961 to be replaced by the next big saloon, the Mark X.

Mechanics

On Mark VIIs the spring bladed tensioner for the timing chains is prone to breakage on the earlier cars. Incorrect tightening of the cylinder heads on these cars can also cause oil leaks. The early Borg-Warner DG automatic gearboxes are known to leak and are difficult to maintain.

Bodywork

With such a massive chassis, these big saloons can survive the ravages of rust. But it's still worth checking the sills, wings, boot and doors.

Spares

Mechanicals no real problem, but body panels rare.

Comments & collectability

Unloved for many years. Potential has been realised today, although rust and neglect has claimed many. Mark IX probably the best practical one to have.

The Mark X & 420G

Production history

Introduced in 1961, the Mark X was a complete departure stylistically from the earlier large saloons. It featured Jaguar's all new independent rear suspension and was initially powered by the E-type's 3.8 litre engine.

In 1962 heated rear window became standard. Mechanical improvements along with contemporary Jaguars were designed to increase efficiency. It also got larger wheel cylinders and larger discs in 1963 to make stopping easier!

The cooling system was uprated in 1964 with the addition of a new radiator. Later that year, along with the E-type the Mark X was fitted with the new 4.2 litre XK and a full synchromesh gearbox.

The Mark X was renamed the 420G (the 'G' stood for Grand) in 1966. The only visible additions to the car was a chrome body strip, new radiator grille and side indicators on the front wings.

The 420G was discontinued in June 1970.

Mechanics

See comments on XK unit.

Bodywork

Like the earlier "Big Jaguars" the Mark X had a certain resistance to corrosion. However, close inspection of the sills (inner and outer), boot, and wings. No separate chassis so rot can be serious.

Spares

Mechanical no problem, body panels rare.

Comments & collectability

A lot of car for your money. Later model the better. Bigger than average Jaguar fuel bills. Not yet regarded as classic, so could be a bargain.

71

The Mark 1 & 2

Production history

The first Jaguar of unitary contruction was the 2.4 saloon. Performance could be boosted by factory tuning modifications.

In 1957 the 3.4 litre was introduced. Effectively this was a Mark 2 Mark 1, with a larger radiator and smaller rear wheelarch spats. Later that year disc brakes were an option on both the 2.4 and 3.4.

These models were succeeded by the Mark 2 in '59. From the outside the window area was increased, a larger radiator grille and built-in spot lamps fitted. The Mark 2 was also offered with the 3.8 litre unit. Inside the instrument layout was completely new, the seats were new and a radio came as standard. Mechanical improvements in line with the other XK engined Jaguars followed.

Ambla plastic upholstery was standardised in 1966 with leather only available as an option.

In 1967 the range was fully revised and just two models were offered, the 2.4 litre 240 and 3.4 litre 340. The models were identical and differed from the old Mark 2 by its slimmer bumpers.

Mechanics

See comments on XK units. Rust attacks rear spring mounting box, and top leaves are prone to breakage. If car appears lopsided this is probably the reason. Heavy brakes means that the servo has gone.

Bodywork

The Mark 1 & 2s suffer particularly badly from the dreaded rot. Wheel spats, front wings, sills and boot. In fact check everywhere.

Parts

Big following means just about everything available, at a price.

Comments & collectability

Mark 2s, particulary the 3.8s are now very collectable. Mark 1s rare because of rust. 2.4s obviously more reasonably priced. Later lower specification 240 and 340 are more affordable.

The S-type & 420

Production history

The S-type was introduced in 1963 and was effectively a hybrid of the larger Mark X and similar Mark 2. The rear was modified to accommodate the independent rear suspension, which resembled a Mark X and at the front there were slimmer bumpers. The S Type was offered with either a 3.4, or 3.8 litres engine.

In 1966 the S-Type was modified and became the 420. It received the 4.2 litre engine with just two carburettors (because of space restrictions). The radiator was more square, with two headlamps on either side. The range was discontinued in 1968.

Mechanics

See comments for XK units.

Bodywork

Comments as for Mark 1 and 2. Basically look in all the usual places, sills, doors, headlamps, boot, etc.

Spares

Again, as for Mark 1 and 2. Although some body panels can be a problem.

Comments & collectability

Scaled down Mark X and some might say more attractive than the Mark 2, and with 4.2 unit a stylish XJ6 alternative. Hasn't yet achieved classic status, so hurry while affordable ones still about.

The E-type

Production history

Introduced in 1961 with the 3.8 litre XK unit as both a fixed head coupé and full convertible (optional glass-fibre hardtop).

The 4.2 litre engine was fitted to the Series 1 E-type in 1964. Detail improvements included uprated brakes, new seats and shorter exhaust tail pipes. In 1966 a 2 + 2 was added to the range which was 9″ longer and 2″ higher. Apart from length, chrome strip on door distinquishes the new model. Borg-Warner automatic offered for the first time on 2 + 2 only.

Interim model unofficially known as the 1½ Series without triplex headlight covers and introduction of rocker switches on dashboard.

Series 2 cars arrive in 1968 and look very different. Larger air-intake, headlamps 2″ further forward, larger sidelights below bumpers, steeper windscreen rake, larger raised bumper, bigger rear lights and safer interior with recessed handles etc.

The E-type gets the 5.3 V12 engine and uprated suspension. Longer 2 + 2 wheelbase adopted but fixed head coupé dropped. 2 + 2 discontinued in 1973 and convertible continues until 1975. Last 50 were finished in black with plaque signed by Sir William Lyons to confirm that fact.

Mechancis

See XK engine guide, but bear in mind that an

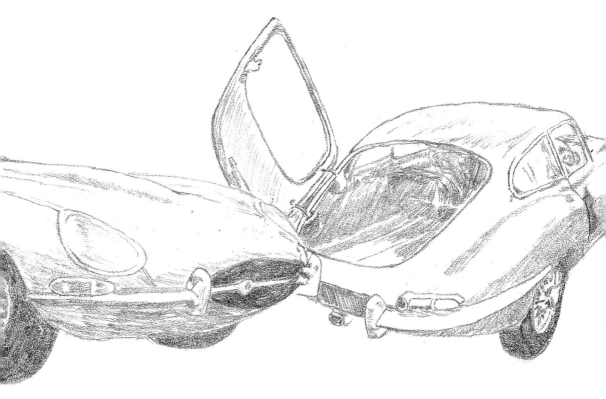

E-type may have led a fast and sometimes furious life.

Bodywork

The E-type is very vulnerable to rust particularly because of its box-section construction. On an obviously unrestored, or average car must be inspected on ramps, or from a pit to assess the true condition. Underneath check the jacking points and sills, watching all the time for bodges such as fibre glass, or extra welded sections.

Look closely at the bonnet, particularly where the wing joins the centre section. Then open the bonnet check for rust and bodges repairs, pay close attention to the headlamp bowls. Doors should be checked, along with the rear wheel arch (including wings on the convertible) and bumper for signs of rust.

On the inside, lift up the carpets and examine where the sill section meets the floor pan.

Spares

Popularity ensures that replacement body panels are about, but they are costly.

Comments & collectability

Roadsters cost more and original 3.8 very rare. Much later 5.3 roadster now equally sought after. No real bargains. Some 4.2 2 + 2s, not everyone likes the high roofline and so can be good value.

The XJ Saloons

Production history

There is a very wide choice when it comes to the XJ saloons. The Series 1 XJ6 was introduced in 1968 with 2.8 and 4.2 litre engine options. Daimler Sovereign variants were introduced a year later. Apart from the the fluted grille Daimlers are distinquished by a more luxuriously appointed interior.

V12 power in the shape of the 5.3 litre XJ12 arrived in 1972. Long wheelbase models were also introduced that year which added a useful 4" behind the door pillar.

In 1973 the Series 2 arrived with a smaller grille, raised front bumper and a larger air intake. The facia was also redesigned. New models included the two door, pillarless coupé in 4.2 and 5.3 engined form. Daimler Vanden Plas offered automatic gearbox, leather upholstery, air-conditioning, electric windows and vinyl roof as standard. The

XJ12 was also badged as a Daimler Double Six. The 2.8 was discontinued in 1975 (to be replaced by the 3.4) and the coupé in '77.

For 1978 the Series 3 had a more noticeable re-style. The roof line was higher, there were black wrap around bumpers, new rear light clusters, fully height adjustable seats and fuel injection became standard.

July 81 saw the XJ5.3 receive the HE engine. Vanden Plas discontinued in '83 and replaced by similarly appointed Jaguar Sovereign.

Series 3 replaced by 2.9 and 3.6 AJ6 engined XJ40. XJ 5.3 Sovereign continues for the time being.

Mechanics

A word or two about the 2.8 engined XJ6 had a reputation for overheating and then

popping a hole in its pistons. Because of this, they are quite difficult to find.

Bodywork

Unfortunately the XJ bodywork can suffer quite badly from rust. Firstly get down on your hands and knees, or if possible jack the car up. At the rear it's the radius arm mounting, rear valance, sills and wheelarches. Body panels can be replaced but chassis members are more serious and more expensive to repair. Moving to the front, check the chassis members that support the engine bay. Other rust points include the boot, so lift the carpet and remove the rear wheel. Bottoms and edges of the doors. Tops of the headlamps, particularly on Series 1 cars.

Parts

Availability very good. Plenty are in the breakers yards and cannibalising two cars might be worth considering.

Comments & collectability

With one exception, at the time of writing there are no indications that the XJ6 is likely to become a valuable investment. Generally manual transmissions are very rare.

Series 1: Few good ones are about so your patience might eventually be repaid if you restore or acquire a nice example. XJ12s built in extremely small numbers.

Series 2: The most common XJ saloon but here you'll find that exception, the coupé. They were made in relatively small numbers and V12 examples are becoming particularly sought after.

Series 3: Being the most recent model it is probably the most practical and refined model to own. At the moment.

The XJS

Production history

The all-new XJS coupé was introduced in 1975 with the V12 power unit. Air-conditioning, electric windows, central locking and radio are standard. Four-speed manual is an option.

In 1977 the GM400 automatic gearbox replaces the Borg-Warner. By 1979 the four-speed manual option is withdrawn.

The new Lucas/Bosch digital fuel injection adopted.

For 1981 the XJS receives the HE package. More luxurious interior includes wood veneer dashboard and leather door casings. On the outside, dome alloy wheels and coachline. For '82 headlamp wash/wipe, trip computer and stereo radio cassette are made standard.

New 3.6 AJ6 engine makes debut in XJS with standard five-speed manual gearbox and limited slip differential. Also convertible version with twin removable targa panels and hardtop and starfish alloy wheels. In July '85 5.3 Cabriolet introduced, but in automatic only. Discontinued 1987.

'88 full convertible.

Mechanics

See comments for V12 units.

Bodywork

Generally the XJS is fairly rust free but lift carpets and check the front footwells because sometimes the air-conditiong drain pipe can become blocked and leak onto the floor. Also, the boot, because of condensation caused by the exhaust, can suffer from rot.

Spares

No problem as still in production.

Comments & collectability

At the time of writing no XJS is particularly collectable, although the first V12 manuals have a rarity value. Most economical and pratical models are the post '81 HEs.

The Daimlers

Production history

For a time after Jaguar acquired them, the Daimler marque did retain its identity with a number of very individual models. But for all models from the 420 Sovereign onwards, see the equivalent Jaguar models.

The Majestic saloon introduced in 1958 with a six-cylinder engine, disc brakes and automatic gearbox. Discontinued in 1962. Similar Majestic Major follows in 1960 but with V8 4561 cc engine. Stretched limousine DR450, went through from 1961 to '68. Replaced by the Jaguar 420G based DS420, with 4.2 XK engine and independent suspension.

Daimler's only roadster the SP250 had a $2^1/2$ litre V8 in a glass fibre body. There was an automatic option and it was capable of over 120 mph. The B models from 1961 had stiffer frame and body. Discontinued in 1964.

The Daimler Sovereign was based on the S-type, using the 4.2 litre XK unit, but with four headlamps and produced between 1967 and '68.

The $2^1/2$ litre mated with Jaguar Mark II body. V8 250 from 1967, has slimline bumpers. Discontinued in 1969.

From 1969 onwards Daimler variants of XJ6 and XJ12 saloons offer more luxury, particularly Vanden Plas versions.

Mechanics

The $2^1/2$ litre unit are prone to bearing wear so be on the look out for a drop in oil pressure.

Bodywork

The original Daimlers are very rust prone. Look just about everywhere for the red peril. For the $2^1/2$ see the Jaguar Mark II.

Spares

With some models body panels very rare. Many specialists for the $2^1/2$ litre unit.

Comments & collectability

All Daimlers have been built in relatively small numbers and those that have survived the ravages of time are real rarities. $2^1/2$ litre's splendid engines make them worth sorting out. As mentioned, Daimlers are cheaper than their Jaguar counterparts, but offer more creature comforts. However make sure that all those creature comforts work, ie electric windows, air-conditioning, etc.

JAGUAR TODAY

Lean years

In 1980 Jaguar was not in the best of health. The products were unreliable and sales were plummeting. Jaguar's reputation abroad was at an all-time low and exports suffered accordingly.

The Series three XJ6 which had been launched at the end of 1979 was well received, with its higher roofline and revised styling of the nose and tail. However, it met with quality control problems and a severe restriction on the number of available body colours.

PROFILE: BOB KNIGHT

Early years

Joined SS in 1943 as a draughtsman from Standard Cars.

Technical achievements

Almost too numerous to include, because Knight had a hand in every post-war Jaguar. Perhaps the most significant is his work on the chassis of the Le Mans winning C-type.

But contributions to the XJ6 in terms of ride, handling and noise supression can never be underestimated.

Management achievements

In 1970 joined the board in charge of vehicle engineering. Appointed Managing Director in 1978, and at a time when all other departments were being absorbed into BL he managed to keep the Jaguar Engineering

Department separate and so retain some independence for the marque. A clever policy of keeping virtually everyone in the dark meant that BL couldn't begin to interfere.

Sum up

When he retired in 1980 Knight had succeeded in handing over a company to John Egan that still had a future. Without Bob Knight there probably wouldn't be the successful company that we know today.

Jaguar reached an all-time low when in April 1980 the assembly line workers went on strike over grading and pay. It was not an auspicious time for their new Chief Executive to join. But John Egan was positively looking forward to the challenge. His first act was to persuade the workforce to set the production lines in motion again.

Revival

As well as beginning to restructure the Jaguar management Egan also set about building a more powerful dealer platform.

Dealers were expected to be up to the mark and earn the right to sell Jaguars. And in the vital North American export market Jaguar talked to dealers there to find out exactly what kind of cars they wanted to sell. The new mood at Jaguar had been set. The cars were about to catch up with the new enthusiasm.

V12 reborn

In July 1981 a revised version of the V12 engine was introduced, known as the HE, or high efficiency. The newly designed cylinder head enabled rapid burning of very lean (petrol) mixtures to take place under a very high compression ratio. Basically this resulted in a more powerful and economical engine. Once installed in the XJ12 and XJS in particular, along with other detail improvements it had the effect of revitalising the range.

PROFILE: SIR JOHN EGAN

Early years

John Egan was born in 1939 and grew up in the Lancashire town of Rossendale. He was educated in Manchester, Coventry and London University where he gained a B.Sc. in Petroleum Engineering. Egan had a head start in the ways of the motor industry because his father was a Ford dealer.

At work

Beginning a career as a petroleum engineer with Shell, he then gained an M.Sc. at the London Business School. As General Manager of AC Delco's UK parts division he proved himself an able businessman. Moving to British Leyland he created perhaps the only success for them during the 1970s at Unipart. But he moved on yet again to Massey Ferguson.

At Jaguar

Apparently it took Egan four months to say yes to the top job. His first words on taking up the appointment were, "One cannot have better ground to build on."

Achievement

In 1983 he was named Midlander of the Year in recognition of his contribution to the success of industry in that area. But the highest accolade was yet to come. The Queen's Birthday Honours list of June 1986 contained a knighthood for John Egan.

New engine – new beginning

As far back as 1980 an XJ57 (modified XJS) was running with an all new Jaguar engine. The plan to replace the ageing, but still effective XK engines in time for the new generation of Jaguar saloons, meant that the XJS would prove to be the ideal test bed for the new powerplant. The AJ6 (Advanced Jaguar 6-cylinder) engine made its 1983 debut in the XJS 3.6 and stylish XJSC 3.6 Cabriolet. This all new engine had an aluminium block, four valves per cylinder and petrol injection.

A chance to share in the Big Cat

Jaguar were now making substantial profits, £49.5 million after tax, production was up above 27,000, over half of which went to North America. Not surprisingly Trade and Industry Secretary Norman Tebbit announced that Jaguar would be sold off. The success of the 1984 flotation was incredible, the demand for Jaguar shares could not be satisfied.

XJ style

Once upon a time you were lucky to get a key fob with the maker's name on it. Today though, Jaguar offer a very wide range of stylish Jaguar inspired products. Everything from a car phone to a tie pin. In fact, the number of products with the leaping cat on them is quite incredible: umbrellas, bags, sweaters, scarves, gloves, ties, sunglasses, belts, leaping cat mascots, carriage clocks, briefcases, suit carriers, wallets, watches, lighters, wedgewood dishes and probably cuddly toys as well.

XJS
Ugly duckling to swan

Heritage

SS100, XK120, E-type.

Development

3 years with Karmann of Germany.

Details

150 body pressings are totally new. Strengthening of structure.

Features

Electronically operated hood. Glass rear window, tinted and heated.

Result

Transformed the controversial coupés styling. Total roof chop a total success. Classic Jaguar, arguably most beautiful since the E-type.

XJ40
a development
diary

1973

Jaguar begins to refer to the XJ40 model as the styling department begin to produce both detailed drawings and clay models. These mock-ups resembled the forthcoming XJS and was scheduled to appear in 1977.

1974

The Italians are coming! Pininfarina, Bertone and Ital Design all had a go at re-arranging the lines on the new saloon. But most of those lines tended to be straight and although fashionable were totally at odds with Jaguar's traditional svelte style.

1975

For a time the XJ40 became the LC40 as Leyland Cars began to exercise their influence over Jaguar.

1976

Styling of XJ6 Series III which would arrive in 1979, contracted out to Pininfarina. Jaguar's styling department manage to cut themselves off from BL and reassert true Jaguar lines.

1977

Sir William Lyons regularly attends secret styling sessions. The feline Jaguar shape begins to return.

1978

An identifiable XJ40 emerges in clay mock-ups. Jaguar Rover Triumph quality car group is established, Jaguar loyalists make sure that the XJ40 project is not stifled, or compromised.

1979

Problems experienced in getting right model body quality from suppliers. Jaguar Rover Triumph is disbanded.

1980

Good news at last! British Leyland give approval a £32.2 million investment in AJ6 engine which will eventually power the XJ40. BL also approve XJ40 concept and 1984 introduction date is agreed.

1981

More money! BL sanctions £77.92 million investment in XJ40 programme. First prototype is built and driven around Brown's Lane.

1982

The new Jaguar takes shape, and in some cases becomes mishapen as a fully engineered prototype is crash tested. The first cars to undergo endurance testing are despatched to Canada.

1983

Severe winter conditions don't give the XJ40 any problems. At the other extreme prototypes were sent to Arizona where air-conditioning and engine cooling could be perfected. In Nardo, Southern Italy, high speed testing proves reliability and leads to gearbox switch. From GM to ZF.

1984

The XJ40 chalks up 1,000,000 test miles. Suggested launch date is 1985, but practical date is 1986. Testing extended to Australia to see how it coped with the outback and New York to test its behaviour around town.

1985

XJ40's launch specification is agreed. Testing continues which now exceeds 4,000,000 miles!

1986

It was worth the wait. 8th October, the XJ40 is officially announced. It receives the UDT/Guild of Motoring Writers "Top Car" award in November.

1987

American launch for the XJ40. XJ6 is phased out. The end of one era and the beginning of another.

JaguarSport

As a result of their success on the race track, the factory are partnering with TWR to produce a more sporting and exciting range based on the existing Jaguars.

At the moment they are concentrating on modifying the handling of the cars, rather than out and out performance.

XJR-S

The XJS has been renamed XJR in tribute to the 1988 Le Mans victory with the first 100 sporting a unique colour, Tungsten Grey Metallic, and trim scheme with stainless steel treadplates that commemorate the success.

Although the power unit remains untouched, the suspension system has been uprated with stiffer front springs, gas filled dampers, modified bushes and rear radius

arms, to improve handling. In addition the JaguarSport 15" Speedline wheels are fitted with Pirelli P600/235/60 tyres.

On the outside, the chrome has been painted satin black and the bumpers are colour keyed, with exclusively designed spoilers and sill mouldings.

Inside, leather sports seats have the XJR-S logo embossed on the headrests, which is carried over to the speedometer and rev. counter. Both the steering wheel and gear shift knob are colour keyed.

XJR 3·6

This is a similar package to the XJR-S, based on the Sovereign saloon, available with four-speed automatic transmission.

On the outside the car looks very different with re-styled spoilers and skirts, satin black grille, all new bumpers that have been colour keyed along with the door mirrors.

Again the suspension is uprated to use JaguarSport dampers and anti-roll bars. The power steering is modified to give improved feel.

Inside the JaguarSport motif is in evidence, complementing the specially trimmed upholstery.

BUILDING
A JAGUAR

What goes into your new Jaguar before it reaches the showroom? Not surprisingly, a lot of hard work. Here's a summary of how they're bolted together.

After the pressing shop has produced the panels the next step is welding them all together. Placed on jigs the welding stations are linked to a quality control centre to ensure that standards are maintained.

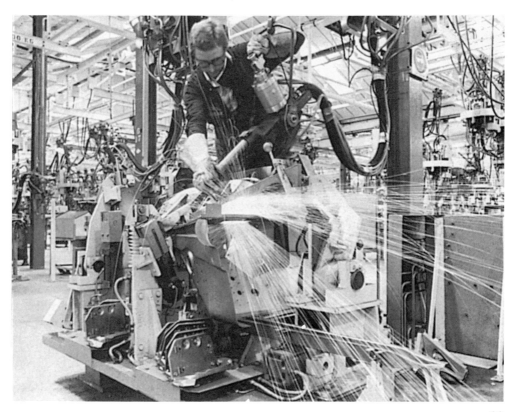

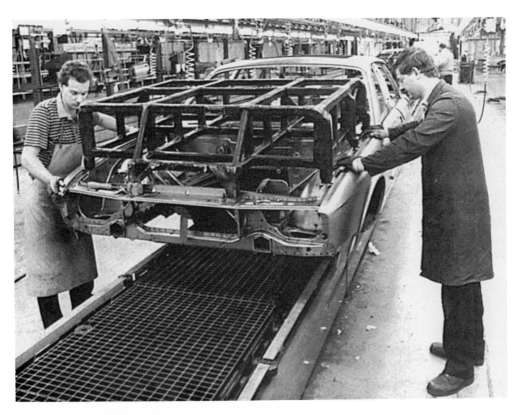

After inspection the body is taken to the build line where the doors, bonnet, bootlid and bumpers are added.

The bodies are then washed in demineralised water and dipped for corrosion protection. The bodies are electro-coated, primed and a surfacer coat added which is then wet sanded. The top coats are then applied electrostatically.

After adding all the electrical items, chromework and bumpers the body is finally mated to the drive train.

Production facts

There are 3 manufacturing plants. 1. Castle Bromwich which produces and paints the body shells. 2. Radford in Coventry which is the engine and transmission plant. 3. Brown's Lane where final assembly takes place. The wood veneer comes from California, from the bole (part below ground) of a 100 year old walnut. It is cut in Germany, then shipped to the UK. 92% of the leather hides come from Sweden and the remaining 8% from Britain. As many as four hides can be used on a single car which are carefully matched for colour, grain and texture, then hand cut and sewn. Every Jaguar engine is hand assembled and then hot run on a test bed before installation.

With the remainder of small components added, the final checking procedures begin. Electrical, rolling road and full road test ensure that the car is up to the mark.

JAGUAR ADVERTISING

"*Swallow*"

From 12 gns.
Write for Cat.

Super-Sports

SWALLOW SIDECAR & COACHBUILDING CO
COCKER STREET and EXCHANGE ST., BLACKPOOL
Tel.: 1011.   Grams: "*Swallow*."

It's 1928 and sidecar prices had been slashed to 12 guineas! These were the small ads that originally appeared in *The Motor Cycle* and local Blackpool newspapers that helped Swallow to grow.

Billing itself as a Swallow Production the SS1 was also promoted as the car with the £1,000 look even though it would set you back just £310.

The value of its beauty
...the beauty of its value !

No car within recent years has received such lavish praise as the S.S. "The car of the year" ... "The car with the £1,000 look" ... these are but two of the many expressions its beauty has evoked. In any company, in any circumstance, the S.S. looks and is distinguished.

And its value is no less striking than its beauty. For both the S.S. Chassis and Coachwork are made in the finest and best equipped factories of their types in the country. No other Speciality Coachbuilder has such an organisation and such facilities. And these are the principal reasons for the outstanding value of the S.S.

The S.S.1. Sports Coupe, as illustrated below, fitted with a 16 h.p. 6-cyl. engine. Ex Works, £310

The S.S.11. Sports Coupe, fitted with 9 h.p. 4-cyl. engine. In appearance, etc., a slightly smaller edition of the S.S.1. Ex Works, £210

See them at any of the many Swallow Agents throughout the country

A SWALLOW PRODUCTION

'Grace Pace Space.' Having invented the sports saloon they also came up with one of the most memorable advertising slogans in history to promote them.

94

More recently the emphasis has been on lifestyle, reflecting Jaguar's growing confidence. But then again they were doing a similar thing in 1933 when the smart thing to do was take a Swallow Hornet to the seaside. And of course many other companies have realised the power of having a Jaguar in their ads and not necessarily for motoring products. Here Pretty Polly prove that 9 out of 10 cats prefer their tights because they're the perfect fan belt replacement.

TRACK STAR. FIVE S

It is, admittedly, difficult to compare the undiluted aggression of Jaguar's Le Mans winning XJR-9 Racing Car with the unashamed luxury of the XJ6 Saloon.

It is, however, entirely appropriate to compare the spirit behind these two vastly different machines.

Uncompromising engineering, and absolute fitness for the job in hand.

For the XJR-9, it means a blend of shattering performance, consistency, and handling characteristics sufficient to wrest one of the most demanding titles in motor racing.

For the X.
the boardroom.
sense of well b
veneer, hand-st
engine managem

PRICES BASED UPON MANUFA

R .

oardroom luxury, away from
less performance. An uncanny
ssurance of polished walnut
ery, together with advanced
iver information technology.

It means enjoying the confidence of driving a sporting saloon
of an impeccable pedigree.

It also means having a sensible regard for the bottom line.

Providing, as it does, a five star
environment for £19,200.

WORLD
SPORTSCAR
CHAMPIONS

CT AT TIME OF GOING TO PRESS INCLUDE SEAT BELTS, CAR TAX AND VAT (DELIVERY, ROAD TAX AND NUMBER PLATES EXTRA). JAGUAR CARS LTD., COVENTRY, ENGLAND

Today they are more than
happy to make the
connection between their
Track Star XJR-9 and Five
Star XJ6 saloon.

An American journalist once
commented that Jaguar's
longest running
advertisements were the C
and D-types. After all, the
odd Le Mans win is
probably the best advert
any company could wish
for, and that trend looks set
to continue.

Here's a selection of tales that are in some cases tall, in others quite true. Others are half remembered, rumoured, or have simply slipped in to recent mythology. But what they all share is a Jaguar, in some shape, or form as the hero of the story.

When one day Evan Davies got four brown envelopes containing a rates demand, lease renewal, electric and gas bill, he knew that it was time to relocate his business. But he would have none of this, Milton Keynes, Peterborough, nonsense.

What Evan wanted was a very special office. It had to be comfortable, have air-conditioning, be cost effective, capable of cruising effortlessly down the motorway and take him safely home at night. What?!?

You've probably guessed by now that Evan bought a car, and not just any old car, but a secondhand Jaguar. He had considered a Daimler Limousine and although that had excellent interior space and headroom, Evan didn't want to feel, or look like the Lord Mayor arriving to open a fete.

The 1980 XJ6 4.2 that he eventually tracked down was in excellent condition and had been maintained regardless of cost. It needed little work to turn it into Evan's fully mobile office for his import/export company. Here's the specification: An extra battery to cope with the extra electrical demands of a busy office. Anglepoise lamps to throw more light on the paperwork. A front passenger seat that pivoted round so that meetings could be held face to face. Split rear seat to give access to the filing cabinets located in the boot. Fold out desk built into the offside door. The customary portable phone, fax machine and computer. A cool box to keep snacks fresh and a very large flask for coffee.

Since Evan started to do business on the

move he's never been so successful. A chauffeur makes sure that he's never late for appointments and a temp handles the paperwork three times a week. He can also work in whatever surroundings he wishes and with the sunroof open he never misses out on a sunny day. He knows the best places to stop for coffee refills, sandwiches and the precise location of every public convenience in London.

But if Evan became too successful think of the congestion a fleet of office Jaguars would cause.

～

We've probably all enjoyed an episode or two of Batman and even admired the original lines of the Batmobile, and from a purely sexist point of view you might have even appreciated the highly original lines of Catwoman. However, the one attribute she didn't have was a car.

The producers had decided early in the second series to find a suitable means of transport for her, and what other car could they choose, but the most attractive cat of them all, a Jaguar.

There was apparently some discussion about the model to be used although the E-type was a clear favourite. The only problem was the production budget which ruled out buying a new, or even an old car. Attempts to borrow an E failed, when it was revealed that the Jaguar would need to be, or subsequently re-sprayed black. Not only that, the design concept also called for some catty additions such as claws, fangs and a tail in the appropriate places.

A Jaguar catmobile would have probably given the dynamic duo's Batmobile quite a hard time. What a shame it was never built.

～

If proof were ever needed that the E-type

Jaguar was and still is the greatest crumpet catcher of all time, Peter Hanway has it. All he needs to do is leave the bright red roadster for a few minutes and when he gets back stuffed under the triple wipers are literally dozens of notes. Not all of them ask for such innocent things as a spin round the block.

And for the purposes of balance the E-type is also a Toyboy catcher. Jocasta Ambury's glacier white roadster gets an awful lot of attention from the young men in her home county of Sussex. Invitations to dinner, night clubs and even offers of marriage are not unusual.

What conclusion can we make from all this? Forget about dating agencies, buy an E-type.

⌒

Robbery is no laughing matter, but it's no coincidence that Jaguars have appeared in a number of films and TV series as the ultimate getaway car.

The Jaguar Mark 2 (as well as S-type) was favoured by the underworld because it was fast and had room for four criminals occasionally more, plus of course the loot. Anything but a Jaguar police patrol car had trouble keeping up.

The most successful, or notorious of all these cars, is still being used as day to day transport by its first law abiding owner in a long time. In fact, she wishes to remain anonymous in case a previous keeper decides to 'borrow' it again for old time's sake.

Built in 1963 the Mark 2 3.8 fell into criminal hands almost as soon as it was delivered, being stolen from ·outside the Jaguar showroom minutes before the customer could collect it. Thereafter the blue saloon fell in and out of getaway drivers' hands for nearly a decade. It was involved in at least 25 robberies that were reported and probably a dozen others where it got clean away. In that time it was resprayed five times and had upwards of twenty registration plate changes.

Apparently just about everyone involved in the felonies was eventually brought to book. Which only goes to prove that crime doesn't pay, unless of course you're making a film about it.

In the film, *Bellman and True* a Mark 2 XJ12 provides the getaway assistance. (Photo courtesy Handmade Films).

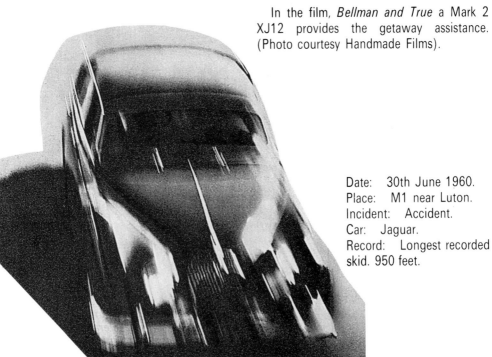

Date: 30th June 1960.
Place: M1 near Luton.
Incident: Accident.
Car: Jaguar.
Record: Longest recorded skid. 950 feet.

Always the bridesmaid but never the bride. A wedding car is a vital part of the whole business of getting married, yet most of the time it gets taken for granted. Unless of course there's a break down. But as car hire boss Fred Smalley totted up the statistics on his most reliable wedding vehicle, a breakdown wasn't one of them.

The Daimler Limousine was recently retired after 20 years service.

Weddings attended: 2,000
Cumulative minutes late for bride (driving round the block): 200 hours
Confetti swept off rear carpets and seats: 1¹/₂ tons
Tin cans strapped to rear bumper after reception: 10,000
Yards of white ribbon: 3,750 yards
Groom never turned up: 4
Bride backed out: 2

Nigel Byles might look like any other sober-suited, respectable and sensible politician on the hustings. But beneath that deceiving exterior lurks the mastermind behind the Let's Have Another Party Party.

With the catchy slogan "Smile Vote Byles" he mounted an incredibly successful election campaign in 1987. As the candidate for Exeter, Nigel had a wide range of policies to woo the voters. Some of them were controversial, others perfectly feasible and several unprintable. To give you an idea of what he had in mind, here's a few headlights from his manifesto.

On the important question of Defence "It wil be creosoted. All nuclear weapons will be scrapped and the money saved invested in Vodka. If the Russians invade Europe we will drop the Vodka on the East Bank of the Rhine and their offensive will grind to a very drunken halt."

I'M ONLY HERE FOR THE BEER!

ELECTION COMMUNICATION FROM NIGEL D. BYLES... YOUR CANDIDATE FOR EXETER

And on the even more important subject of Drink "Pubs and wine bars will be allowed to open 24 hours a day, seven days a week. All taxes on booze will be scrapped. Pensioners will receive a weekly drinks allowance." And when it came to Leisure "Stonehenge will be renovated and the roof put back on it. Terry Wogan will be sold to the Libyans."

As for Transport "The M5 will be re-cobbled south of Bristol. the Channel Tunnel will start in Exeter, and be 300 feet high to allow planes to use it in bad weather." However, the news for Jaguar owners ran as follows "All Jaguar cars are to be painted British Racing Green until such time as they win the Le Mans 24 hours race. And anyone caught driving a Porsche will also have it painted British Racing Green."

Were the 'Let's Have a Party Party' clairvoyant? And how would Jaguar owners have reacted to having their Old English White, or Squadron Blue cars being transformed? Unfortunately we will never know because the LHAPP only found 200 people sensible enough to vote for them.

During the 1930s SS cars had their typewriters fitted with a special key that produced the SS symbol.

Call Peter Byebury eccentric if you like (though he could throw a punch at you), but he's a totally committed Jaguar owner. So much so that he always makes sure that his Old Jaguar goes to a good home when he sells it.

Having run and enjoyed Jaguars for nearly 30 years from XKs to XJs, he can afford to be fussy as Peter is now the successful owner of a large engineering firm. This means that he has the resources and option to buy-back any of his old cars when the owner has finished with them. Now if that sounds strange, just look at the selection process that a potential buyer of an ex-Byebury Jaguar has to go through. Byebury has to be given a £1,000 cash deposit from which he will deduct expenses whilst investigating the suitability of the buyer.

1. The buyer's garage must have an independent form of heating and be large enough to accommodate the Jaguar.
2. Undertake to clean the Jaguar every week and steam clean every other week during the winter months.
3. Service the car at a Jaguar franchise or engage the services of a Jaguar trained and qualified mechanic.
4. The buyer must have the personal resources to maintain the Jaguar, which will be verified by reference to the buyer's assets.
5. Never transport dogs, or unaccompanied children.
6. Members of the Institute of Advanced Drivers will be given preferential consideration.
7. The Jaguar can only be insured under a comprehensive policy.
8. Only the buyer's immediate family are allowed to drive the Jaguar.
9. The right is reserved to buy back the Jaguar at a fair market price once the owner has decided to sell it.
10. Breach of any ownership condition will

(a)

(b)

(c)

PASS
☐

FAIL
☒

PASS
☑

FAIL
☐

PASS
☐

FAIL
☒

result in the immediate forfeit of the Jaguar without compensation.

You might have noticed that these conditions read like a legal document. Well in fact that's just what it is. Mr Byebury had his solicitor draw up this contract which the buyer is obliged to sign.

So far Byebury has not had to repossess a Jaguar and surprisingly in view of the restrictions there's no shortage of buyers.

Probably one of the most remarkable and longest running Jaguar stories can finally be pieced together.

In 1964 Milton Waxman, a chain store

owner from Texas received an interesting present from his Mexican suppliers. They were grateful for his orders over the years and had noticed that he always showed interest in their Mark 2 saloon which was used as a run-about. Or rather Milton would have received this interesting present if it hadn't been for the intervention of a small Mexican airline.

Flight 881 had its usual cargo of fresh fruit and its unusual cargo of a very well used Mark 2 Jaguar. But the Dakota aircraft was starting to have trouble almost as soon as it took off. The starboard engine was having a particularly hard time of it giving the pilot palpatations as it spluttered in and out of life. Not surprisingly the plane started to lose height and would have had difficulty making it over the dense South American jungle if certain items hadn't been jettisoned in time.

Of course, the Jaguar was one of the first things to leave the cargo door and Milton never got to see his Jaguar.

Moving forward a decade to 1974, a party of American scientists and ecologists were exploring the Mexican Jungle when they came across a curious sight especially in the middle of a tropical rain forest. An almost perfectly restored Mark 2 Jaguar. It had been placed on a raised platform and was surrounded by fruit and orchids.

Consulting the local Indian population an interpreter discovered that the Jaguar was a focal point of worship. The real jaguar had alway been respected by the Indians and they had recognised the mascot on the bonnet. And anyway when it had arrived in the forest, so had a bumper crop of fresh fruit which meant that it brought good luck.

The fact that it was in good condition is explained by the denseness of the trees which broke the Jaguar's fall. And as the Indians were expert craftsmen fashioning gold into statues and jewellery, repairing and panel beating the damaged areas wasn't a problem.

The American team left the Jaguar where it was. However, this ad appeared in a British newspaper recently. Could it be the same car?

To quote Sir John Egan: "The Jaguar is an animal of great beauty, agility and distinctiveness – characteristics we have always sought to embody in the cars we produce."

You can't disagree with a statement like that, but the fact is that jaguars are now an endangered species. Consequently Jaguar Cars are launching a project to create the world's first jaguar reserve in Cockscomb Forest, Belize in Central America.

Leading the project on behalf of the World Wildlife Fund, Melanie Watt a graduate in Zoology from Toronto University commented: "We will be using the money to set up the Cockscomb Reserve and ensure that it is managed effectively by trained and properly equipped rangers."

And as about 500 jaguars live in Belize, at least 50 of them do so within the reserve area which makes it the highest known concentration of these big cats almost anywhere.

Without Jaguar's help the jaguar could become extinct within the next decade. Let's hope that never happens.

Jaguar facts

Can weigh 400 lb and grow up to 7 ft long.
Hunts close to and in rivers.
It's a very strong swimmer.
Zoologists call it the Jaguar Panthera Onca.

CELEBRITY JAGUARS

Famous owners

One of the first signs of success is a nice car. But people who buy Jaguars don't do so just to show off. It's a car with a seemingly endless list of qualities. The photos on these and following pages show a famous few who've owned Jaguars for many different reasons.

Jaguars on film

They pop up just about everywhere on TV and at the cinema on and off the set in the company of the famous.

Other Jaguars on film and TV include, **The Italian Job** – 3 E-types get crushed by a JCB and tipped over a ravine. *The Equalizer* – Sovereign Saloon is Edward Woodward's avenging transport. *Minder* – Arthur Daley takes a break from his dodgy forecourt in an XJ6. *To the Manor Born* – Peter Bowles, the man next door had a Lynx Eventer. *The Saint* – Simon Templar sped around in a white XJS. *Fletch* – Chevy Chase almost got to set an XJS alight. *The New Avengers* – Steed had a highly modified XJ12 coupé. *The Sweeney* – Jaguars were always the getaway cars. They only crashed in mid-chase so that Regan and Carter could catch up in their old Granada. And many, many more.

Egon Ronay As the man behind *The Good Food Guide, Good Hotel Guide, Good Restaurant Guide* he could probably write The Good Car Guide after travelling many thousands of miles on research missions. The Racing Green XJS V12 he regards as his best Jaguar after having owned Sovereigns in the past. And of course the XJS takes him swiftly and comfortably between appointments without the need to stop off at motorway service stations! [Autocar & Motor]

Wayne Sleep After a hard evening treading the boards, world famous dancer Wayne Sleep likes to relax in the back seat of his Daimler Limousine. If you're in any doubt, that's the car on the right. The one on the left is a Fiat Gamine Vignale and not surprisingly has been christened "Noddy", whilst the Daimler is, yes you guessed it, "Big Ears". Previously the property of the Maharishi and apparently bought for him by a Beatle, it was registered in the name of "The World Government for the Advancement of the Age of Enlightenment". The Daimler replaced a Bentley for the simple reason that it gave Wayne more room to stretch his tired legs! [Sunday Times]

Joe Loss Purveyor of the finest big band music from the '30s and '40s has been a Jaguar owner for just as long. But in those days they were known as SSs. The number plate on his 4.2 Daimler Sovereign was actually acquired by accident. [Autocar & Motor]

109

Steve Cauthen Earned his nickname 'The Six Million Dollar Kid' when he came to Britain from the States as a teenager and proceeded to win every race in sight. Driving 60,000 miles a year to races means that it's important that he arrives in a relaxed state. Not surprisingly the XJ40 performs this job admirably, although Steve has got his eye on another mount. A Jaguar XJS! [Autocar & Motor]

Peter Purvis & Simon Groom Anyone who makes a living out of old Squeezy bottles, sticky-backed plastic and silver milk bottle tops must want to drive home in something more substantial at the end of the day. This is certainly the case with these two ex-Blue Peter Boys. Peter Purvis was running a well used Daimler 4.2 when this picture was taken. His policy is to run a stylish car without the penalties of depreciation. Simon Groom is a much more committed Jaguar fan. The Mark 2 2.4 in the picture was purchased whilst his S-type was being restored because he simply couldn't bear life on the road in anything but a Jaguar! [Autocar & Motor]

David Steel The ex-Liberal Party leader debunks the image of a boring politician by being a committed old car enthusiast. His fleet recently included a big Mark IX, but that was swopped for the more economical Mark 2 2.4. Apart from the obvious advantages of owning a Jaguar, for Mr Steel it has the added benefit of being instantly recognised in the constituency. And when it comes to election time, what do the voters think of first, the Jaguar or Mr Steel?

Chris Difford When he's not having hit records with Squeeze, Chris Difford can be found exploring the countryside behind the wheel of his splendid Vicarage Mark 2. This most British of cars is utterly appropriate for the member of Britain's best pop group. 'Up the Junction'. I don't think so.

George Formby One of Britain's most popular entertainers and film stars was an early customer, investing in a two-tone SS1 in the 1930s. The registration plate was incredibly prophetic and read 'XJ 7171. The Mark VII he owned in the '50s bore the legend GF 2.

Steve McQueen An avid collector of both cars and motorcycles, he apparently had an escalator installed in his house to take them upstairs!, film star McQueen owned an **XKSS**. Being an accomplished driver, he almost always did his own stunts, McQueen could easily appreciate the qualities of the rarest Jaguars of them all. [Autocar & Motor]

Michael Aspel The Six O'Clock Show, Aspel & Co, Ask Aspel, Childs Play. Without doubt he's one of the most successful and popular TV personalities around. However, the switch from a Daimler Sovereign Double Six to the more confined XJS V12 didn't prove so popular with his mother-in-law. [Sunday Times]

Robert Kilroy Silk Former Labour MP and TV presenter, Robert Kilroy Silk has always needed motor cars that he could rely on. In the main he has owned continental cars simply because British ones have rarely offered the quality, or reliability. Except that is for Jaguars. However, the final choice was made for him by his family who all insisted that an XJS convertible would be perfect. And of course it is.

A young Monarch shares a joke with William Lyons on her official visit in 1956.

The Duke of Edinburgh enjoys a drive in an XKSS.

113

This XJ6 was locally
converted in 1972 for the
Queen's tour of Mauritius.

The Duke of Kent takes
delivery of a new 3.4 Mark
2.

Not only is this the first all-steel Jaguar, the lucky owner was King Carol of Romania.

Bob Hoskins and Jaguar in *Mona Lisa* (Photo courtesy Handmade Films).

Clark Gable Hollywood star Gable was always a very loyal Jaguar customer. Handing over the new XK 120 with additional radio and special wheel trims, is William Lyons.

Elizabeth Taylor & *Michael Wilding* More Hollywood stars who knew that the most stylish car on the boulevard was always a Jaguar drophead.

'Sweet Devil' *Bobby Howes*, well known all-round entertainer in the '30s with one of the pair of $1^1/2$ litre saloons which were featured in the film.

Withnail and I Two very out of work actors living in squalor reckon that the grass is much greener and more profitable in the countryside. And the only way to get there is in a Jaguar Mark 2 MOT borderline. (Photo courtesy of Handmade Films).

Mona Lisa Out of prison and into a very different world. The only thing he can rely on of course is his Jaguar Mark II, offering many a quick getaway. (Photo courtesy of Handmade Films).

Bellman and True A smashing time for a Series 2 Daimler Double Six especially after a highly lucrative bank raid. (Photo courtesy of Handmade Films).

JAGUAR
bits and pieces

Here's a selection of unusual, rare, strange and sometimes bizarre Jaguars, that quite honestly didn't fit neatly anywhere else in the book.

Jaguar pick-up

Yes that's right, this is a Jaguar pick-up. Based on a Mark 2 3.8 it was built by West German Peter Keiselt. But don't get upset that a good old Mark 2 has been hacked about just for the sake of it. When Peter found it, the Jaguar was in a very sorry state indeed and worth just a handful of marks.

However, the possibility of a practical pick-up intrigued Peter and 18 months later this beautifully proportioned hybrid emerged.

Any resemblance between the rear "shelf" and the top of a grand piano is not entirely co-incidental because Peter builds and restores pianos! Not surprisingly, much of his skill and craftsmanship went into building this Jaguar which was the key to his success, and led to this *grand* result, but of *chords* you can see that the *lid* has really been lifted on this *major* Jaguar *concerto*, sorry conversion that . . .

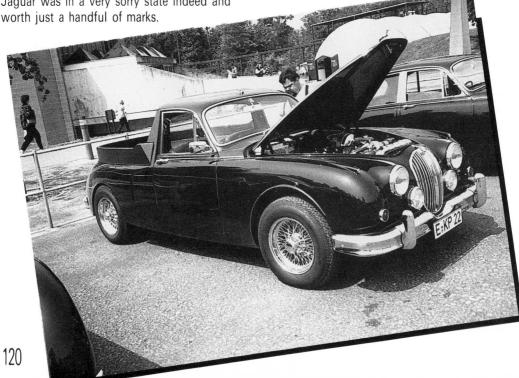

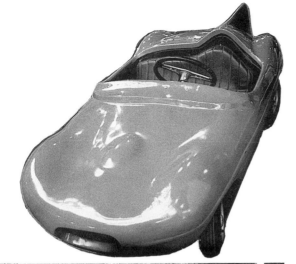

The smallest Jaguar part I

If this reminds you of a D-type that has shrunk in the wash, you're not entirely wrong. Part of the cat family it was known as the Cheetah Club. In 1963 it would have set you back £112 10/-; not an inconsiderable sum in those days.

Powered by a 75 cc Villiers motorcycle engine this little rocket would power up to a top speed of 14 miles per hour. This car's main claim to fame is that one was owned by Russian Premier Kruschev's grandson!

Smallest Jaguar II

This might look like any other well cared for XK 120, but if you take a close look at the two ladies in charge, you'll notice that they're on the young side. Therefore the scale of this perfectly formed Jaguar is on the small side.

Built to special order by Autotune Limited this children's sports car has a fibreglass body and is just 73 inches long by 31 wide. Like any good Jaguar the seats are leather, although the big break with tradition is the rear mounted engine. This unit is a Briggs & Stratton 4 stroke that is more normally to be seen powering lawnmowers.

What's more, this is an affordable second Jaguar that could easily fit into the boot!

Smallest Jaguar III

Now, does this sight take you back or what? Assembled here is probably the definitive collection of diminutive Jaguars. Triang, Corgi, Dinky, Matchbox. Where are they now? In the loft? In the shed? At the back of a cupboard? Probably passed off to the Oxfam shop years ago.

The thing is that these old toys are being taken seriously as collectors' items and are worth a great deal of money. So hadn't you better start rummaging around the attic? (photo courtesy of Mint & Boxed).

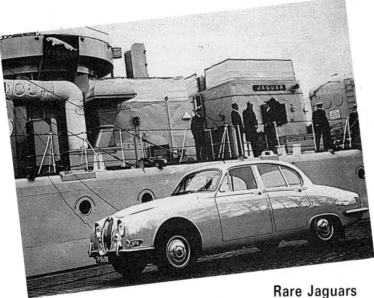

Rare Jaguars

Jaguar photo opportunities

The name Jaguar stands for a lot of things, including speed and style. It's fair to say that Sir William Lyons' cars are almost totally responsible for this. Of course, everyone else has since got in on the act. But in order to promote the cars, posing an S-type with HMS Jaguar, or pairing up some E-types with the Jaguar Jet is an opportunity that never went begging.

Just about everything produced by Swallow and SS before the war is incredibly rare, but there are several examples that are especially sought after.

SS90 was introduced in 1933 with a 2.7 litre engine and close ratio gearbox. The prototype (above) had a rounded tail, although the production cars featured a flat tail on which was mounted the spare wheel. Based on a shortened SS 1 chassis the styling was classic Lyons although the performance

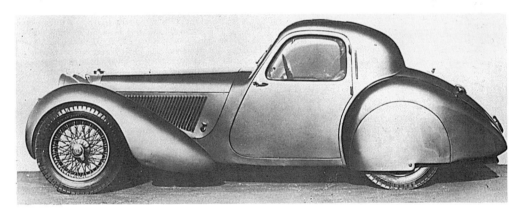

was disappointing. Not surprising the SS100 that followed shortly after was a more satisfying and potent package, but the SS90 had paved the way. Just 23 were built.

The SS Airline. The first and last time that Jaguar followed fashion. In 1935 many manufacturers were trying to follow the American trend towards aerodynamic styling. It could almost be described as a fastback or 2 + 2 coupé these days. Never a popular model in the SS range. Only 600 cars were produced.

SS100 coupé. Built as a one-off for the 1938 Motor Show this prototype was never put into production. However, it is possible to see the close resemblance between this and the XK 120 coupé.

Rare racers

Car: XJ13.

Name: The 'XJ' stood for experimental Jaguar.

Dates: Designed 1965. Finished 1966. Tested 1967.

Purpose: Acted as a test bed for a V12 XK power unit.

Technical: (i) Engine – Four overhead camshaft producing 500 bhp from close on 5 litres. (ii) Chassis – monocoque. (iii) Suspension – E-type.

Styling

Malcolm Sayer who developed the D and E-type's lines. Conceived as a coupé it ended up as a targa without the top.

Secret

Although this looked like the perfect weapon for Jaguar's return to Le Mans, the factory was careful to keep the car quiet.

Record

Unofficial testing did take place in 1967 and racing driver David Hobbs lapped the MIRA circuit at 161.6 mph, faster than any other car.

Crash

Sadly a tyre failure sent the XJ13 into a tumble. Driver Norman Dewis was fine, but the car had to be rebuilt.

Sum up

One of the most exciting Jaguars ever produced, but wasn't, if you know what I mean. Perhaps the XJ 220 will make up for it.

Nickname

Brontasaurus.

Date

1953.

Purpose

A Lyons styling exercise, apparently to keep the Competition Department on its toes.

Style

It has to be judged a failure when compared with Lyons' classics. Especially as the enclosed front wheels meant that it couldn't be steered.

No records

However, it was intended as a record breaker where turning corners isn't so important. Although it had a few outings, there were no serious road attempts.

Jaguar 'Jeeps'

Names: VA and VB.
Purpose: A project that SS Cars took on during the war. These lightweight off-road jeeps. Intended to be parachuted into battle zones.
Technical: VA was powered by a V-twin JAP motorcycle engine and the later VB by a more powerful Ford 10 unit.
Advanced: These Jeeps incorporated many interesting features that wouldn't be seen on production cars for decades, such as independent suspension and unitary chassis/bodywork construction.

Jaguar fire engine

As well as the appropriate number plate and useful ladder, notice the familiar leaping cat on the grille. Jaguar to the rescue!

Jaguars on the water

Once afloat, the XK engine was just as effective as on dry land. Miss Windermere with Norman Buckley at the helm was probably the best known, setting many records. A succession of similar boats have followed. The factory did take an interest, producing 'The Legend' a twin turbocharged power boat. But that interest waned once they had returned to the track in 1985.

JAGUAR

RECORD BREAKERS

Car: MG EX.135.

Power: 2.0 litre 4-cylinder Jaguar XK unit.
Driven by: Lieutenant Colonel 'Goldie' Gardner.
Location: An Autoroute at Jabbeke, Belgium.
Date: September 1948.
Record: 176 mph.

Car: XK120 coupé

Drivers: Johnson, Fairman, Hanley and Stirling Moss.
Location: Montlhéry, France.
Date: August 1952.
Records: Numerous class and World records, at 10,000, 15,000 kms and 10,000 miles. Over 7 days and nights it covered 16,851 miles.

△

Car: XK120

Modifications: Virtually none, apart from 'bubble' over the driver.
Drive: Norman Dewis.
Location: Jabbeke, Belgium.
Date: October 1953.
Record: The intention was to create some publicity for the motor show. The top speed was an impressive 172.412 mph.

▽

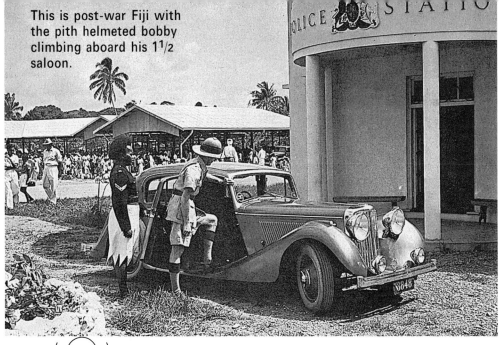

This is post-war Fiji with the pith helmeted bobby climbing aboard his 1½ saloon.

Police
JAGUARS

On the principle that it takes one to catch one, Jaguars have always been a popular choice with the constabulary. The association goes back a long way.

These officers look pleased with their new Mark IV, until they realise what needs to be loaded into the boot.

Incredibly this is what a motorway patrol Mark 2 had on board, 'just in case.' It's a wonder they could catch a speeding push bike with all that in the back.

The XJ6 carried on where the Mark 2 left off and was a daunting sight in your rear view mirror. At the time of going to press the XJ40 was being evaluated by the police, but unfortunately it may not be a cost effective proposition.

Powered by Jaguar

Many companies have produced cars based around Jaguar's superb engines. Some of them have even attempted to better Sir William Lyons classic designs, but often with limited success.

Lister Jaguar

At the heart of this racing car is an XK engine. HWM, Cooper, Tojeiro all produced similar Jaguar based specials which dominated British racing in the '50s and '60s. Rather than being poor cousins of the real cats they were regarded as thoroughbreds in their own right, attracting some of the best drivers of the day such as Stirling Moss, Duncan Hamilton, Peter Whitehead, Peter Walker and Ivor Bueb. Archie Scott Brown who was regarded as the best driver of this generation, steering Listers to many fine victories (Photograph courtesy of Sotheby's).

Panther

The intension of Bob Jankel was to create cars that echoed the classic sports cars of the '30s whilst utilising modern components. The J72 was clearly an SS100 lookalike and was initially powered by the 3.8 XK, before taking up the 4.2.

With the De Ville, Panther aped the Bugatti Royale, a massive limousine pulled along by Jaguar's V12.

130

Miscellany

Bertone rebodied an S-type in 1966. Jaguar engineers liked the car enough to propose limited production. But the BMC merger ends such dreams.

Eleven years later they decided that a modern Jaguar Sports Car ought to look like a Lotus.

Micholetti used a D-type chassis for this coupé. Seen for the first time at the 1963 Geneva Motor Show.

American car designer Raymond Loewry obviously had a very individual view of the direction Jaguar should take in 1955.

Farina built this 'Flying Jaguar' known as the Meteor in 1952. There was a convertible version called the Golden Arrow.

Rapport, builders of exotic and customised machinery for anyone who could afford expensive cars, asked designer Chris Humberstone to produce something for them based on the XJ6.

Stripped of its body Kevlar composite wings, steel doors, aluminium bonnet and bootlid were added. Originally conceived as the Forte with interchangeable roofs to change it from a coupé to a convertible, spyder or estate the receiver stepped in to halt production. Just two versions, an estate and

convertible were built.

If any coachbuilder's attempts should have been built it was this beautiful example from Pininfarina in 1978. Based on the XJS it remains as enticing could have been, with two piece hood, deformable nose and tail sections and electronic instrumentation.

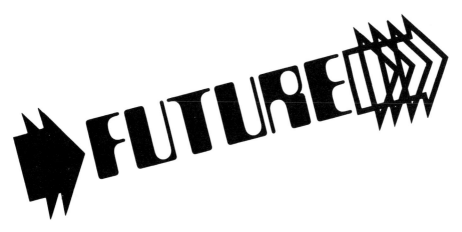

Jaguar are building for the future with their recently opened engineering centre, sited just six miles from Brown's Lane. Vehicle design, advanced engineering, vehicle and component development, vehicle safety, compliance and engine testing are all accommodated at this new facility.

In short, a car can be taken from an original idea through to computer design, then clay mock up and finally a fully operational prototype. The Whitley Engineering Centre: Jaguar racing green is used on the exterior of this ultra modern complex.

Styling Department

27 Designers/Computer Aided Design/ Computer Aided Modelling/New vehicle concepts.

A new Jaguar model, being modelled.

Development department

60 Engineers/Product legislation and com-
pliance/Vehicle safety/Vehicle Electronics/
/Chassis/150 engineers – Power unit and
transmission/24 Engine Test Cells.

Whitley facts

150 mph top speed on largest rolling road.
£55 m spent annually on development.
155 acre site.
500,000 sq feet of development space.

Testing rigs simulate five years of ownership in hours. But what new cars are going to emerge from this new centre, and who's going to be responsible?

Achievements: Part of the team which developed the XJ12 Car of the year 1972. Prepared the document which provided funding for the XJ40. Accepts top car award in 1979 on behalf of his colleagues for the XJ40.

Future: Many projects underway, developing existing XJ40 and more specialist sporting Jaguars. Committed to preserving the Jaguar's reputation of elegant design combined with excellence of engineering.

Name: Geoff Lawson.
Position: Chief Stylist.
History: Trained at the Royal College of Art. Worked for General motors designing Vauxhalls and later commercial vehicles. Joined Jaguar in 1984.
Achievements: XJS Convertible. XJ40 restyle.
Future: Currently working on a variety of styling projects, F-type, XJ40 & XJS restyles. Very aware of the Jaguar heritage and is seeking to emphasise the traditional "cat-like" sleekness in the new designs.

Name: Jim Randle.
Position: Director of Product Engineering.
History: Came from Rover in 1965 to become chief vehicle-research engineer. Succeeded Robert Knight in 1980.

135

What new cars will Jaguar produce to take them into the 21st century?

XK-F The XJ41 Sports Car projects is set to be the E-type for the '90s. More of a sports car than the XJS, whilst the former remains in production. Roadster and coupé versions are likely.

XJ42? Could Jaguar with its increased production capacity cater for the obvious demand for a smaller Jaguar. There was certainly no shortage of customers for the Mark II in the '50s and '60s so why not a BMW 3 series beater for the '90s?

XJ40 Apart of detail restyling in the '90s Jaguar have been known to have experimented with a number of different body styles from a pillarless coupé to an estate car.

XJS will also look different in the '90s. An officially produced estate version similar to the Lynx Eventer, would be very welcome.

Jaguar Sport

It will be their job to produce exciting versions of the future range, in low volume, but very high quality and probably entirely new concept vehicles.

Motorsport

Jaguar having restored their competition pedigree with the XJRs, the rumours are that the leaping cat symbol could soon be found on the flanks of a Formula One Car.

And of course any speculation on Jaguar's racing future couldn't exclude Tom Walkinshaw. His plans are ambitious and, if his record of success is anything to go by, we can look forward to even more Jaguar's taking even more chequered flags.

Codename XJ 220

Development

Conceived by Jim Randle as a Group B road racing concept in early 1985. A team of twelve Jaguar designers and engineers worked on the project in their own time. By early 1987 the style had been established; the next stage was to move from a $^1/4$ scale model to full prototype. With the co-operation of specialist suppliers.

Power

6.2 litre, 48 valve V12 producing more than 500 bhp.

137

Transmission & suspension

A four-wheel system handles the power with a sports like double wishbone set-up. The specially developed ABS system is designed to cope with 4WD.

Performance

Maximum Speed 200 mph + 0–100 mph in 8 seconds.

Bodywork

Unitary construction made of bonded aluminium incorporating a steel roll cage. All outer body panels are made of aluminium. Bonding processes are 'top secret.' The doors swing up to allow entry, and a switch on the fascia provides powered door closing. The rear spoiler can be adjusted by the driver.

Extras

This is a luxury car finished to the highest standards. heated front and rear screens, air-conditioning, electric windows, infra red remote central locking, electrically heated seats with electric lumbar support, a CD player with graphic equalizer and five position steering column.

Production

The project has been passed to JaguarSport for evaluation and production looks almost certain at the time this book went to press.

Sum up

Really showing what Jaguar can do. In some ways an appropriate full stop for the Jaguar Driver's Book it is also the best indication of the exciting things that Jaguar are likely to do in the future.

Owners' & enthusiasts' clubs

If you're fanatical about Jaguars and want to know more about them, help is at hand. In fact there are thousands of other enthusiasts all over the country who feel exactly the same way as you and they are all members of the many specialist Jaguar clubs. You don't even have to be a Jaguar owner, just absolutely nutty about the cars and everything that goes with them. Imagine whole weekends, looking around, talking about and arguing over Jaguars. Newsletters that keep you up to date with Jaguar activities. As well as access to rare parts special insurance schemes and discounts.

So here's a brief summary of the specialist clubs who cater for Jaguars and Daimlers. It's up to you to decide which club is right for your needs. Simply write to them and they will, without obligation, send you all the information that you'll need.

Formed in December 1984 the club caters for all Jaguars including the Daimler derivatives. They are committed to keeping all their members' cars roadworthy and have formed a Spares Liaison Committee to organise a parts location service. Not only that, a full Spares Department has also been established along with a technical advice service.

Other services include a rescue scheme, vehicle assessment, motor & mechanical breakdown insurance, books and Club accessories and regalia. There is also an award winning monthly magazine which covers the technical aspects of ownership, including spares and restoration information. Members can also submit their own contributions.

They organise a full calendar of events both on a local and national basis with 37 regional and international (Cote D'Azure, Belgium, Denmark and Hayling Island!) centres.

Contact: FREEPOST
Aldershot
Hants
Surrey GU12 4BR

The Club is open to all enthusiasts of the Jaguar marque. A magazine is produced every month and contains news about Jaguars from all over the world. Social events are organised on both a local and national level. In fact, the Club has more than 30 local centres around the country. Technical advice is always on offer.

Seven registers represent the interests of individual Jaguar models from SS to XJ. A Competition Committee organises race meetings and test days for members at race circuits all over the country.

Contact: Jaguar Drivers' Club,
Jaguar House,
18 Stuart Street,
Luton LU1 2SL.

This is the newest Jaguar club formed in April 1988 and made up of many ex-Enthusiast Club members.

It is open to all owners and enthusiasts of the entire Swallow, SS, Jaguar range including Daimler and other derivatives. They organise, social, motor sport and other events both regionally and nationally. They are forging links with similar clubs all over the world.

They hope to establish the Sir William Lyons Foundation for the benefit of everyone interested in the life and work of Jaguar's founder.

Contact: Richard Pugh,
19 Eldorado Crescent,
Gloucestershire GL52 2PY.

The Club was founded in 1964 and covers all Daimlers and the Jaguar based derivatives (or is it Daimler based Jaguar derivatives?).

There's always a busy programme of rallies and special events on both a regional and national basis.

They help to maintain Daimlers by offering a comprehensive spares location service. There is also a monthly magazine called *The Driving Member* to which members are encouraged to submit contributions.

Contact: John Ridley,
                FREEPOST,
                The Manor House,
                Trweyn,
                Abergavenny,
                Gwent, NP7 5BR.

This is not a complete directory of every Jaguar specialist but it should include at least one or two companies who may be able to help you find that elusive part, finish that attempted restoration and perhaps make it move just a little more quickly, or even supply a kit that could transform your Jaguar!

The following symbols should help you quickly identify what they get up to:

OA	OB	OC
Performance	Bodykits	Replica kits
OD	OE	OF
Restoration	Spares	Scale models

*Inclusion in this section does not necessarily imply recommendation of the companies concerned as neither author, or publisher will be aware of managerial changes, or policy after publication.

Kearns Richards Service Ltd (OE)
Atlantic Street,
Altrincham,
Cheshire WA14 5DD.
061 928 2897
Engine specialists. Parts.

Lynx Cars Ltd (OA/OB)
68, Castleham Road,
Castleham Industrial Estate,
St. Leonards-on-Sea,
Sussex, TN32 9NU.
0424 51277
Performance. Bodykits, etc.

Olaf P Lund & Son (OE)
2–26 Anthony Road,
Saltley,
Birmingham B8 3AA
021 327 2602
Spares.

Paladin Jaguar (OE)
51A Bell Street,
Reigate,
Surrey RH2 7AJ
0737 241100
Parts.

Midland Jaguar Centre (OE)
Bryant Road,
Bayton Industrial Estate,
Exhall,
Coventry CV7 9EN
0203 362947
Parts. Repairs.

Mk2 Services (OE)
Inglewood Garages,
Inglewood Road,
London NW6
01 435 2832
Repairs, service and engine.

G.H. Nolan Ltd (OE)
1 St. Georges Way,
London SE15
01 7701 2785/2669
Spares.

Peter Neal Engineering (OE)
Unit 5 South Down Industrial Est,
Harpenden,
Hertfordshire, AL5 1TW
05827 62424
Parts. Repairs.

Peter Thurston (OD/OE)
Hanover Street,
Herne Bay,
Kent, CT6 5RN.
0227 373438/374402
Restoration. Parts.

Phillips Garage (OA)
206 Bradford Street,
Deritend,
Birmingham B12 0RG.
021 772 2000
Performance.

SC Jaguar Components Ltd (OE)
13 Cobham Way,
Gatwick Road,
Crawley,
West Sussex, RH10 2RX.
0293 547841
Parts.

Normal Motors (OD/OE)
100 Mill Lane,
London NW6
01 431 0940
Spares, repair & restoration.

Sherborne Engineering (OE)
Unit 6, Douglas Close,
Preston Farm Industrial Estate,
Stockton-on-Tees,
Cleveland, TS18 3SB.
0642 67744
Repair. Parts.

Southern Classics Ltd (OD)
MWG House,
Hanworth Lane,
Chertsey,
Surrey, KT16 9LA.
0932 567671
Repair. Restoration.

DJ Sportscars International Ltd (OC)
2 Edinburgh Place,
Edinburgh Way,
Harlow,
Essex, CM20 2DJ
0279 442661/2
Dax Tojeiro Kit.

Ottercraft Ltd (OC)
5 Foundry Lane,
Hayle,
Cornwall, TR27 4HP.
0736 755016
Steadman TS 100 Kit.

Robin Hood Engineering (OC)
64–74 Mansfield Street,
Sherwood,
Nottingham.
0602 608371
RS Daytona Kit.

Ronart Cars Ltd (OC)
102 Dunsberry,
Bretton,
Peterborough PE3 8LB
0733 268295
W152 kit.

Steven Channels Mk 2 Jaguar Spares
(OD/OE) Unit 1, Hamlet Hill,
Roydon,
Essex CM19 5JY
027979 3670
Parts. Restoration.

Three Point Four Jaguar Services (OD/OE)
Fitzwilliam Street,
Summer Lane,
Barnsley,
South Yorkshire S70 2NL
0226 292601
Restoration. Spares Mk 2.

Kougar Cars Ltd (OC)
Overlook
Budletts,
Uckfield,
West Sussex TN22 2EA.
0825 2800
Sports Kit.

Duncan Hamilton Ltd (OA/OB)
The Square,
Bagshot,
Surrey, GU19 5AX.
0276 71010
Arden Performance & bodykits.

Guy Salmon Ltd (OB)
Portsmouth Road,
Thames Ditton, Surrey KT7 0TA.
01 398 4222
Body styling.

Janspeed Engineering Ltd (OA)
Castle Road,
Salisbury,
Wiltshire SP1 3SQ.
0722 21633
Performance. Bodystyling.

C.F. Autos (OD)
5 South Road,
Erith,
Kent.
0322 346584
Repairs & Restorations.

Classic Engineering (OD)
503 Southbury Road,
Enfield,
Middlesex EN3 4JW.
01 803 5534
Restoration.

Autocars (OE)
Rawreth Industrial Estate,
Rawreth Lane,
Rayleigh,
Essex SS6 9RL
0268 782306
Parts

Chris Coleman (OE)
17 Devonshire Mews,
Chiswick,
London W14.
01 995 9833
Spares.

David Manners (OE)
991 Wolverhampton Road,
Oldbury,
West Midlands B68 4RJ.
021 554 4040
Parts.

Focus Engineering (OD/OE)
Unit 5, Plot 21,
Bellbrook Industrial Estate,
Bell Lane,
Uckfield, Sussex TN22 1QL
0825 67620
Restoration & Spares.

Four Point Two Motors (OD)
Unit 6,
Claggy Road,
Kimpton,
Hertfordshire SG4 8QB
0438 833434
Restoration.

Jag Nuts (OE)
Hazelfield,
South Warnborough,
Nr Basingstoke,
Hants RG25 1RZ.
0256 862364.

FB Components (OE)
35–41 Edgeway Road,
Marston,
Oxford OX3 0HF
0865 724646
Parts.

Forward Engineering (OA)
Walsh Lane,
Meriden,
Warwickshire.
0676 23526
Performance, race prep.

Grange Motors (OE)
2 Brook Street,
Brentford,
Essex, CM14 5LU.
0277 260793
Parts.

Jagspares International Ltd (OE)
Beeston Industrial Area,
Kings Lynn,
Norfolk, PG32 2NQ
0328 70151
Spares.

Jaguar Spares Specialist (OE)
Paxton Mill,
Scitcliffe Street,
Accrington,
Lancs BB5 0RG.
0254 398476
Parts.

Proteus Reproductions (OC)
Albert Street,
Little Lever,
Lancashire. BL3 1JH
0204 709465
Proteus C & D Type Kits.

Mint & Boxed (OF)
42 Watford Way,
Hendon,
London NW4 3AL.
01 202 8186/7
Models.

Jaguar Specialists (OE)
36 Druid Street,
London SE1 2EZ.
01 403 7272
Parts

Silhouette Cars (OC)
Unit 14, Rutherford Court,
Brunel Road,
Earlstrees Industrial Estate,
Corby, Northants NN17 2SJ
0536 67755
SC 500S Kit.

Grand Prix Models (OF)
167 Watling Street,
Radlett,
Herts.
09276 2828
Models.

TWR Group Ltd (OA/OB)
1 Station Field Industrial Estate,
Kidlington,
Oxford, OX5 1JD.
08675 71555.

Vicarage Cars (OD)
13/1 Stanmore Industrial Estate,
Bridgenorth,
Shropshire WV15 5HR
0746 766031
Better than new Mk.2 & E-types.

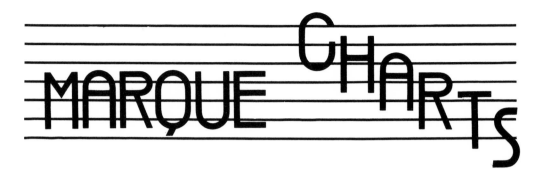

Now if you wondered what model replaced which and when, these Jaguar Marque Charts should help. They could even settle an argument with a fellow Jaguar fanatic. On second thoughts though, they might even start several nasty incidents if my research is wrong! Oh yes, and there's also a chart for Daimlers too.

I've put in as much detail as possible without bogging you down with every single version or derivative. But make sure that you take notes because questions may be asked later during the Trivia Test.

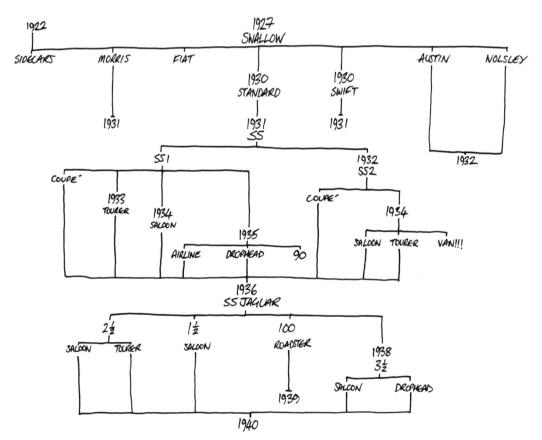

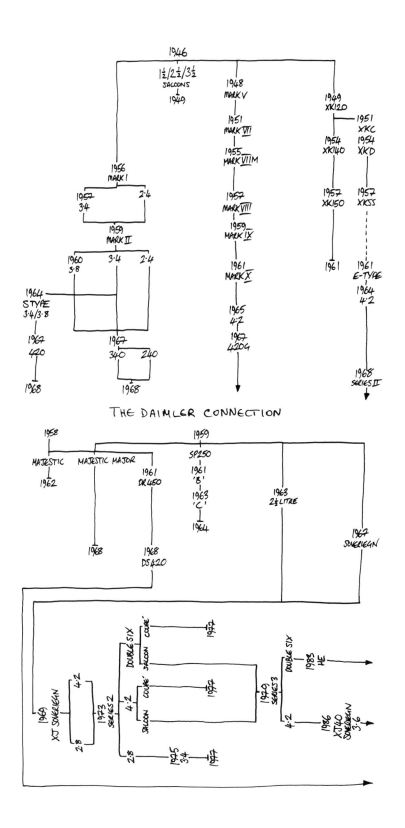

THE DAIMLER CONNECTION

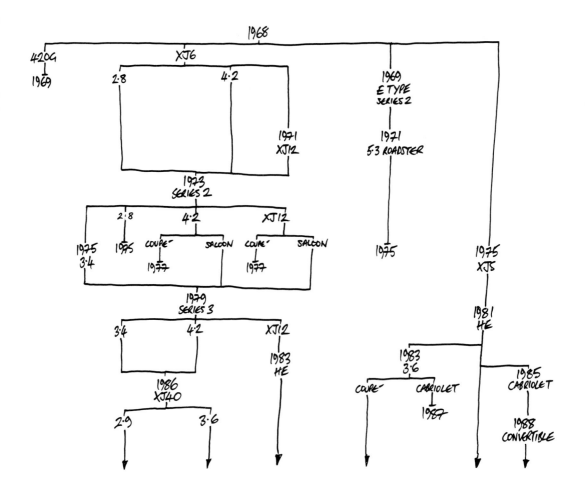

1968

420G
1969

XJ6

2·8   4·2

1971
XJ12

1973
SERIES 2

2·8   4·2   XJ12

1975   1975   COUPÉ   SALOON   COUPÉ   SALOON
3·4

1977   1977

1979
SERIES 3

3·4   4·2   XJ12

1983
HE

1986
XJ40

2·9   3·6

1969
E TYPE
SERIES 2

1971
5·3 ROADSTER

1975

1975
XJS

1981
HE

1983
3·6

COUPÉ   CABRIOLET

1987

1985
CABRIOLET

1988
CONVERTIBLE

148

JAGUAR

QUIZ

TRIVIA

Here it is, the moment you've been waiting for. The end of the book. However, it isn't quite over yet. Why not pit your wits against Professor Gustav Foresight who came up with this brain tickling quiz. All the teasers contained here are based on the information contained in the Jaguar Driver's Book, so there's no excuses.

1. True·or False. (i) The XK 120 was so named because it took 120 days to design and build. (ii) Jaguar didn't build an all steel car until 1937. (iii) The E-type was once described as 'The greatest crumpet catcher of all time'.

2. What did these styling mock ups eventually become?

a.

b.

c.

What does 'XJ' stand for?

5.

In what film did (a) Bob Hoskins have a Mark 2 as his trusty transport? (b) Some desperate bank robbers demolish a green house with a Daimler Double Six? (c) A pair of degenerates take a Mark 2 to the countryside?

a

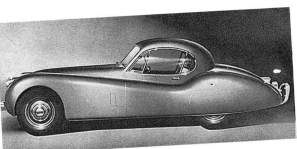

c

$$a+b \div c \times d = ?$$

d

6.

Who are they? What have they done?

7. What are the family connections?
Identify these racing Jaguars.

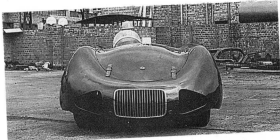

a.

b.

c.

8.

Across
1. Adorable (2) saloon. (3)
2. Built just one. (1) (2)
3. Second Home (2) (4)
4. First Home (8)
5. Every Jaguar needs them (7)

Down
1. Roadster headgear (3)
2. Life without, unthinkable (5)
3. Fast part of slogan (4)
4. The family (4)
5. C, S, E, D, (4)

9. What's the connection between these two?

10. What comes next?

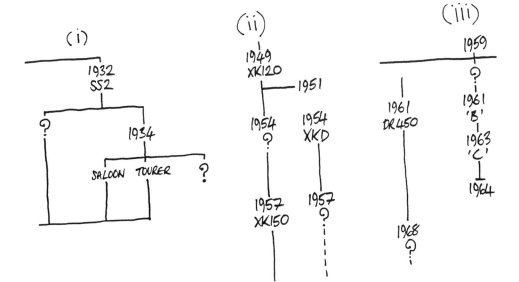

(i)

1932
SS2

?

1934

SALOON   TOURER   ?

(ii)

1949
XK120

1951

1954
?

1954
XKD

1957
XK150

1957
?

(iii)

1959

?

1961
DR450

1961
'B'

1963
'C'

1964

1968
?

(overleaf for ✓ or ✗)

THE SOLUTIONS

How to score. One mark for each correct answer which includes a mark for each sub question and every crossword line you solve.

1. (i) False. (ii) True. (iii) True.
2. (a) XK 120 (b) Mark VII (c) XJ6
3. Experimental Jaguar.
4. (a) Mona Lisa. (b) Bellman and True. (c) Withnail and I
5. 420 + 120 ÷ 240 x 8 = 18
6. Ian and Pat Appleyard who have just won the Alpine Rally. Pat was the daughter of William Lyons.
7. (a) Brontosaurus. (b) C-type 'long-nose'. (c) XJR-5

9. They are both powered by V12 Jaguar engines with the XJR-S in the foreground so named to celebrate the victory at Le Mans.

8.

154

10.

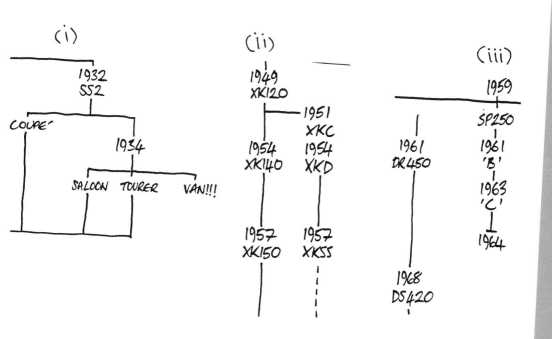

(i)

1932
SS2

COUPE'

1934

SALOON   TOURER   VAN!!!

(ii)

1949
XK120

1951
XKC

1954   1954
XK140   XKD

1957   1957
XK150   XKSS

(iii)

1959

SP250

1961   1961
DR450   'B'

1963
'C'

1964

1968
DS420

How did you score and what does it all mean?

0 – 10 Seek medical attention. You really can do a lot better than this. Back to page one.

10 – 20 Congratulations, you're not as stupid as you look. A respectable score, but you're certainly no Einstein. Make sure you take notes next time you thumb through the Jaguar Driver's Book.

20 + Cheat. If not, you're head is likely to have trouble negotiating doorways, Re-read the book, but don't pay too much attention this time.

It's often difficult to keep up with the pace of change in the motor industry and this book is no exception. Between completion and publication there have been new models, products and developments. Here's a selection of the most important events that give valuable pointers to the future of Jaguar cars.

Project XJ-40

To mark the £200 million cost and seven years of development that went into building the new XJ6, a permanent exhibition has been staged at Coventry's British Museum of Road Transport. Entitled Project XJ-40, it features two development vehicles and fully engineered cutaways of the 2.9 and 3.6 litre units.

In addition, videos and photographs illustrate the car's progress from the drawing board through to production.
(By kind permission of the Museum of British Road Transport, Coventry)

156

XJR-10

A successor to the Championship-winning XJR-9 made its debut in the American IMSA race series in the middle of 1989. Another Tony Southgate designed racer, it is lower and powered by an all-new engine. The JRV6 is an alloy, four-valve, twin-cam, twin-turbo unit. It features a smoother nose, slimmer engine cover and larger ground-effect tunnels.

RIP Daimler Limousine

It's the end of the road for the long-serving Daimler Limousine, beloved of funeral directors, wedding hire companies and Lord Mayors. Production will cease in the early

1990s. A specialist workforce of just 50 built around 200 of the cars each year.

No reasons have been given for terminating this profitable car's existence. Indeed a rescue bid was mounted by two businessmen, Colin Highams (former racing driver and head of Hooper Coachbuilders) and David Backinsell. To get round the problem of using the Daimler marque outside of the UK, which is licensed to Daimler-Benz, they proposed reviving the Lanchester name, still owned by Jaguar. Their intention was to take over production in their own works near to Brown's Lane with the existing workforce. Even though they designed an all-new car, at the time of writing the Limousine is to be discontinued without a successor, or prospect of revival.

Lister Le Mans

To celebrate Jaguar's 1988 Le Mans victory, WP Automotive have produced a very special edition XJ-S. Like their other models, this is an entirely reworked car, from the engine right through to the bodywork. But rather than simply being Le Mans by name, it has the same racing nature as the XJR-9s. With a 200 mph top speed, it could almost keep up with Jaguar's official racer.

6.0 litre XJR-S

Launched by JaguarSport this model replaces the 5.3 V12. The new 5993 cc power unit delivers 318 bhp at 5250 rpm. That means an electronically limited speed of 160 mph and a 0–60 time of just 6.5 seconds. It also utilises a new automatic gearbox designed specifically for the 6.0 and Zytek sequential injection and digital ignition engine management system developed direc-

tly from Jaguar's Group C racing programme. In addition the suspension has been uprated and the car features new 16 inch Speedline wheels and new ZR rated Dunlop high performance tyres.

On the outside, this new model can be distinguished by the discreet badges and optional satin finish chromework.

XJ6 1990

Jaguar have introduced a whole host of changes for the XJ6 to see the range into the next decade. The most significant is the introduction of a 4.0 litre version of the AJ6 engine. There is also a new four-speed automatic transmission, Teves ABS brakes, and catalytic exhaust system. Inside there is a revised analogue instrument pack, simplified trip computer and detail design changes. Sir John Egan, Chairman and Chief Executive puts the range in context:

"I believe our 1990 Model Year car is essentially a new generation XJ6, the effect of the changes is that fundamental. We have enjoyed great success with the XJ6 range since launch, but our mission is one of constant improvement. I think that we are succeeding in that mission, and it has been achieved by listening to customers and setting ourselves ever stiffer targets."

AND FINALLY

The XJ220, Jaguar's brilliant and beautiful 220 mph supercar is to go into limited production. A total of 350 cars is to be produced, each at a price of £360,000.